To dear Hall.
Enjoy u
love, Jeannie
x

© 2018 Ella Sheepcote
Between the Covers

Ella Sheepcote asserts the moral right to be identified as the author of this work.

All rights reserved. No part of this publication may be reproduced, stored in a retrieval system, or transmitted, in any form or by any means, electronic, mechanical, photocopying, recording or otherwise without prior permission of the publishers.

Published by: ©Art Noise
Layout and cover design by: ©Art Noise
Cover illustration and images by: ©Art Noise

ISBN: 978 1727568356
Printed and bound in United Kingdom
Lulu Press, Inc. – www.lulu.com

Between the Covers

ELLA SHEEPCOTE

For My Special Friend.

CHAPTER ONE

Ella sits outside the library and coughs unexpectedly; the taste in her mouth is bitter, clear phlegm lands in her tissue. This is the after effect of choking back tears that Patrick the Piscean has released by sending her a text.

'Your attitude towards Anneke is childish. People have noticed the glares you've given Anneke and my wife. You were rude to my wife. My son told me. I still love you but if you want to come down I suggest you get the asp, or is it the wasp, out of your arse. And as for your literary friends, they're a bore to my intellectual brain.'

Ella had packed his things, washed the sheets and restored the room for her grandchildren to sleep over. Sleep had evaded her, but she had breathed deeply and probably managed to doze for a few hours.

Anneke, his café assistant, has in recent weeks ignored Ella, not even acknowledging the hellos or goodbyes, apart from one time when Ella glanced over at Anneke. Their eyes met and she remembers her saying, 'Ella, don't look at me like a cow.'

'I'm not,' Ella replied, and avoided looking in her direction again. She didn't want a scene. Did her glance linger just a little bit too long? She stared at the table and fiddled with her spoon, polishing it with a serviette, got some papers out of her rucksack.

As for Patrick's wife, they were separated. The only time Ella was curt to her was when he'd not opened his previous premises, the café bar, on time. His son was standing outside phoning him. There was no response from Patrick. She felt a sickness in the back of her throat. His estranged wife arrived soon after, asking, 'How are you?'

She muttered, 'Fine,' but tears were welling. She needed to escape and rushed down the street. No answer. It reminded her too much of Tony going missing. She tried to breathe. Her breaths were short and rasping. A walk by the sea was the solution. Then later she went back. She checked the café bar was open and that Patrick the Piscean was okay.

The last remark about the literary group in his text was suspect. He had enthusiastically listened to contributors, so why be so hurtful? Ella had negotiated the extra business. Was this how Patrick showed his gratitude? It was probably excess whisky, that provoked the text, but that was no excuse.

That morning she calls a taxi. The bags are too heavy to haul on the bus – all Patrick's detritus gone in them. Apart from the radiator key; that might come in useful sometime. Typical, he is late. The café isn't open yet. So, she finds herself hiding in a little alcove by a shop, near the café, in case his estranged wife drops him off – unlikely but not impossible. She's shivering. She's taken her vitamins but not had breakfast.

Ella had planned to dump his stuff and say, 'Have a good day!' and just go. Now she is in the position of a furtive woman with a couple of large shopping bags, trying to be invisible. She attempts to peek out from time to time. Every car that passes makes her uneasy. Eventually she sees his lanky figure turn the corner. She breathes a sigh of relief. He's on his own. She waits for Patrick the Piscean to put his keys in the lock. He looks drawn.

'I've brought your stuff.'

'You shouldn't have bothered.' His breath smells of whisky.

'Well you promised to collect it and didn't. I need to know what's happening.'

Patrick takes the bags from her, puts them down. Ella goes to leave.

'I'm going now; you've got your belongings.'

'You can't just go like that.'

'Yes, I can.' She starts to shiver uncontrollably.

'Just sit down a moment.'

Compliant as ever, she sits, rather than just walking away and protecting herself.

Patrick makes some take-away coffees for customers. Ella automatically gets up, spying the dead leaves on the poinsettias. She cannot stand dead leaves or dying flowers since Tony died. Dead things are a constant reminder of decay. A decaying body not found.

She hears Patrick say, 'I'll make you a cup of Rosie Lee then, if you want, you can join me on the bench outside.'

She nods her head. She is feeling shaky, goes back to the chair. Minutes later they are sitting outside.

He's saying, 'You could have controlled your emotions. You could have been reasonable about Anneke. I was really happy when you came to the café, and then I got your text about Anneke and everything changed.'

'You know I don't lie. I felt it right in the pit of my stomach. It made me feel ill.'

Then the tears fall, like torrential rain. She hears herself stuttering 'sorry' intermittently. Why is she saying sorry? She's done nothing wrong? She looks at the blue sky, patched with white clouds, the chimney pots, feels the salt tears pour down her cheeks and her stomach churning. Her whole body is heaving, with waves of sorrow bursting out. It is no use – she can't stop. Now she doesn't even care. The hurt has burst, stifled for too long. It flows freely. It reminds her of the widows' tears poured into glass bottles and then sealed, which she'd seen in an exhibition about the First World War.

'Can I please have some sugar?'

'Sugar?'

'Yes sugar. I need sugar. I didn't sleep well. Sugar!'

She's shaking. She's in shock. She can't stop trembling. Patrick gets her sugar.

From time to time he goes in to make people their drinks, but explains how he has an upset customer outside and needs to sit with her.

She hears him repeatedly say, 'Emotion is good.'

Then intermittently, 'Breathe deeply, deep breaths.'

He mutters, 'I'll soon be dead.'

'Why in the hell are you saying that?'

'It's a joke.'

'That's sick.'

She wails even more and says a line she's been rehearsing at home. 'You know, you are not the one. I need someone who will protect me, give me time, be there for me. I deserve that.'

He's releasing a dam that Ella has suppressed for years. He will have to deal with the consequences. Patrick the Piscean sits with her in silence, witnessing her outburst. Her howling eventually subsides to sobs. She goes inside and he follows.

'Can you make me some toast. I feel as though I'm going to be sick. I need to eat,' adding 'please' and 'thank you', something drilled into her at boarding school.

'Of course.'

Ella sits as waves of nausea wallow in her throat. She swallows, tells herself it will be okay and goes to the toilet. She breathes deeply, washes her hands, dabs her eyes, and exits. A customer she knows comes in.

'How are you Ella?'

'Fine,' she says with a fixed grin.

'It looks as though it's going to be a nice day.'

'Yes, the sky is getting bluer, but the wind's chilly.'

'It's a bit burned, I'm afraid; but it's the way I like it,' confesses Patrick the Piscean.

'Never mind.'

Ella doesn't care – she just needs food. Now. He scrapes off the burned bits, and spreads it with peanut butter. He doesn't have any Marmite, but he knows peanut butter is her next favourite spread and hands her the plate. Ella eats the fingers of toast and the retching stops after the first few mouthfuls. Soon afterwards, she gets up to leave.

'Where are you off to?'

'To the Centre. I'm running the games club.'

'Just cancel it, you should rest.'

'People are relying on me, I have to go. I can't let them down. Bye.'

'Take care.'

Luckily there is a bus just coming to the stop, around the corner from the café, that will take her to opposite the Centre. She slumps down in her seat.

****

Ella loves to express herself in clay, earth and paint. They form patterns in her mind. Finger nails are not pre-filled with soap. Grime can't easily be scrubbed out. The rawness of the connection with Patrick the Piscean has unlocked a font of feelings she'd unknowingly coffined in grief. She makes marks, outlines, letters that form words that spill into sentences, hoping to understand her physical desire, unravel the threads. She wants to release her hurt and find wholeness.

Words pour out, sometimes rain down, in the form of tears after drought. Water brings Ella Earth, like clay, to life. She enjoys the feel of squishing the clay in her hands. It retains her unique finger prints. Ella is searching for a balance between earth-clay and water. She constructs her story as she would a clay vessel.

****

CHAPTER TWO

Ella arrives just in time, sets up the Scrabble, and gets some scrap paper and a pen so David can write down the scores. A few minutes later Simon and David arrive. The other group are already playing Upwords, similar to Scrabble, but you can build up and cover the letters to a maximum of five letters high. The boys prefer Scrabble, and as a volunteer she's offered to play with them so the others are free to enjoy Upwords.

She says, 'I must warn you it's been a difficult day and I'm feeling tired.'

'Are you feeling alright?' Simon enquires

Dreadful. But she knows focusing on something neutral will help her calm down, not allowing her to be overwhelmed with self-pity, an undignified emotion.

'Yes, but I didn't get much sleep. Never mind, choose a letter to see who'll start the game.'

Will she be able to cope? She reassures herself that she always does.

Ella picks 'P' (how ironic, 'P' for Patrick the Piscean), and the boys 'E' and 'S'.

'So, who goes first?'

'The one with 'E'.'

'E' like your name Ella,' says Simon.

That's right. It reminds her of Patrick and her playing Scrabble on one of the evenings when he stayed with her, at his temporary home. She reminisces about how she got out the box, one she'd found in the market.

'It's probably one from the sixties,' he'd commented

Patrick likes old things. Well, he liked her, didn't he? She isn't a thing, of course. She goes on to think how he didn't really want to take his stuff out of his room. Well, he'd procrastinated, left it there. She was going to wait until after his dad's funeral, but the vituperative text had made her take action.

Yet she recalls with fondness his voice encouraging her when she got a good word playing Scrabble, praising her, something she appreciated. Now, what were the words? She remembers some of them:

raw, warm, moods, sip, id, quip, bile, stretchy, erect, eke, fuck (the c being a blank), hug, moist, mate, nature, navel, jive.

They were poetic, found words, and they had slipped into her unconscious. Patrick had scrawled 'Winner!' on the top of the paper. He'd also realigned the words, so each of the letters were straight, a little foible. He liked geometric lines. It was a pleasant evening – more than pleasant. Ella really enjoyed the evening.

She is pulled back into the present, 'So what's the score, Ella. Can you help?'

One of the boys has covered a red triple-score square and the letters added up to nine points.

'Three times nine is twenty-seven.'

'That's good isn't it?'

'Yes, very good.'

Ella concentrates on helping them play the game and her mood settles.

She sees and hears Simon's fingers tapping.

'Please Simon, can you try not to tap. It's distracting.'

'What does 'distracting' mean?'

'It means it's annoying,' said David.

'It's putting me off,' Ella replied.

She thinks of Patrick's mum being annoyed by his father's constant tapping.

'I'm sorry, I was thinking about my family,' Simon mutters.

David answers, 'Don't think about your family; box it all up. It only makes arguments in your head and you get angry.'

Strange, that both she and Simon are thinking about families. Well, she's thinking of Patrick's parents, but then she reminds herself to stay focused.

'What films do you two like?'

'Comedy films,' Simon replies.

'And Ella, what sort do you like?'

'Feel-good films or based on true stories.'

'I like action movies,' David says.

Ella answers, 'Personally I can't deal with any sort of violence.'

Simon starts tapping again, she gently touches his fingers.

'I shouldn't be tapping, is that what you are saying?'

Ella smiles, 'Yes, please stop tapping if you can. That would be really kind of you.'

'Sorry, I didn't mean to upset you.'

That's fine. Now, whose turn is it?'

'It's mine.'

'Well, Simon, let's see your letters; take the 'O' and put it under the 'B' and then put the 'X' below the 'O.' Now what does that spell?'

'Box.'

They finish their game.

'Thank you for coming and I hope you both have a good week.'

Simon says, 'Sorry if I annoyed you and I hope you'll feel better soon.'

Ella finds herself smiling.

It might be stupid, but she feels drawn to go back to the café. Yes, the café is a place she feels at home. She questions her motives, but automatically finds herself going in that direction. It's part of her routine, structure. Does she want to continue another disastrous relationship? She's had two already; her first husband, Robert, and then Tony, her second.

Robert, her first husband had taken Susan, his mistress, away for the weekend early one Saturday morning. She remembers looking out of the window. He'd said he was going on a conference. Ella saw Susan come out of the block of flats diagonally opposite. He kissed her on the cheek, took her bag and put it in the boot; something he never did for her.

When questioned later, Robert answered, 'Why did you look out of the window? I was trying to protect you.'

'Why, for Christ's sake, couldn't *you* have driven around the corner?'

'You shouldn't have looked.'

She shakes her head. Tony wasn't innately bad, but his mental health meant he could be brusque, even rude. She dealt with his occasional psychotic episodes. When she tried to reason with him, he would strangulate her words, literally bruising her throat so she would gasp for air, not knowing when her next breath would come. Yet she survived. He was always truly sorry afterwards.

Ella has never knowingly given into fear, but is this stupidity? Does she really want to be hurt again? She panics outside the café. She comforts herself with the thought that she is back because it's like falling off a horse. Ella wants to be where she knows people relate to her, apart from Anneke, that is. And why be intimidated by her?

Ella has every right to be there. She wants to show she is brave, or is it compassionate, kind; or perhaps a combination of both?

It was like Tony travelling by train the day after he'd been taken ill. A Swedish student had pulled the emergency cord thinking Tony was having a heart attack. It was a seizure. He got no warning, or so little, just a second's foreboding, a feeling of sickness in the back of the throat. The next day people chose to stand in the corridor, rather than sit in his compartment. The Swedish girl, however, saw him on the train and was delighted he was fit enough to travel. Fit, but he didn't 'fit' in.

Ella goes into the café where Patrick is surprised, 'Hello, it's so nice to see you.'

His smile gives her confidence. She's done the right thing.

One of her café friends, Andy, comes over to her and asks how she is.

'Well, it's been a bit of a shit day to tell you the truth. Two acquaintances died recently, and there is a possibility of the Centre where I volunteer being closed.' Ella was concerned. She wanted the Centre that had supported her after Tony's death to continue to help people. She didn't mention her upset with Patrick in the morning.

Patrick comes with her soup; roasted pepper, tomato and harissa, with brown bread.

'Here you are – it's just been made. Would you like some butter?'

'No thanks, I'm trying to be good.'

'Anneke made it.'

Patrick goes back into the kitchen.

Andy puts his arm round her waist and gives her cuddle, something he's never done. She's really grateful and stifles the tears as she eats her soup, which is warm, thick and tasty. She's dipping torn bits of crusty bread, 'ducks' as she called the floating pieces as a child. She dunks them in the deep pink liquid, trying to erase resentment, nurture herself.

When she leaves, Patrick is being distracted by another customer. She probably won't see him before his dad's funeral and knows he's worried about writing the eulogy, that's the reason why he drank the bottle of whisky.

'I'll be thinking of you on the fifteenth. I hope it goes well.'

He looks up, 'Thanks Ella, take care.'

'Bye, Patrick. And Anneke.'

Only Patrick acknowledges her leaving.

Ella knows her tears still aren't far away. They drizzle spontaneously from time to time. She has a local radio programme to do later and walks to the nearest park. She enjoys the spring bulbs. As she gets there she sees Marcus, a man she's met a few times before. Tears start to fall. He opens his arms wide and embraces her. She is apprehensive and too scared to hug tightly because of his back operation. He hands her some tissues.

'Sorry, I have been upset by a friend. Sent me a horrible text. He was drunk. I was hurt and told him so.'

'It's good to say the truth.'

'I can't stop crying.' Ella blows her nose. They continue walking in the park.

'Being here in the green, in nature, is soothing,' he says.

They look for a café with comfortable seats. Marcus needs his back hugged in a padded chair. She suggests a place and, sure enough, there are two leather, curve-backed comfy chairs in the window. It is the same café where the community radio studio is housed.

He has a latte, she a chamomile tea, and they chat.

'The operation left me in a half reality.'

'It must have been difficult.'

'Eventually, I woke from this sort of stupor. Now my head is clearer. I can go swimming again.'

They get onto the subject of death. Well, he tells her his chances were fifty-fifty of waking up after the spinal procedure. It took seven hours to remove the growth and put rods in to shore up his spine. She tells him how Tony, her second husband, had committed suicide; sees his mouth tighten, his eyes looking dolefully at her, 'I'm so sorry.'

'He'd had many attempts. I knew immediately, when the policeman knocked on my door. Now I feel I have to really celebrate my life, that's what he'd have wanted.' She regrets spewing her own stuff out so she adds, 'I saw the film *Coco* about The Day of the Dead, in South America. It's a cartoon but very good.'

'Interesting, the Anglo Saxons are bad at dealing with death. They celebrate Halloween, for children, but not All Souls, which observes our mortality.'

'The Japanese also celebrate a day when the dead come back. They put out the photographs of deceased relatives, friends, together with their favourite food; and light candles.'

Marcus starts to move his neck gingerly from side to side massaging it gently with his fingers, 'Friendships are one of the most important things in life.'

Ella knows that, whatever happens, she wants – no, she needs – the thread that was being woven like an invisible root between her and Patrick to survive. It is a balm, like the lemon balm in her garden, which surprises her when it hits her nostrils, refreshes her spirit. Yes, he calls her a 'romantic', and maybe she is. She can't bottle him – he would smile at the pun – she can only savour his food, his repartee, his embrace.

She looks at Marcus's eyes. They're flickering. He's walking up and down now, arching his back, so she asks, 'Would it best to go home now?'

He nods and smiles. She is about to stretch out her arms for a goodbye, when she senses any unnecessary movement would jar his back even more. He leaves.

Before going down to the radio studio, she meets her lovely Turkish friend, who runs a charity. He loves women, poetry and cats – not necessarily in that order. He normally hosts the radio programme before hers. Tiredness overwhelms her; her eyes want to close, doze, and her limbs want to slump. She tells him about her day and he hugs her.

'The bad things will go,' he says, 'the echo remains, but then fades.'

She sees him after the show and he clasps her head, strokes her hair saying, 'Go home, switch off your phone and relax.'

She smiles, knowing he works all hours and hardly ever sleeps and, to relax, watches cat videos.

****

Handling the tiles inscribed with letters, thinking of possible word formations within set geometric lines refocuses Ella's mind. It soothes her. It's like her hands, rather than her mind, rhythmically preparing, repetitively kneading the clay, using her core muscles. Her gut instinct relishes that familiar movement. In the process she will discover some foreign bodies but they will be expelled as her hands pummel. This process saps her strength.

She seeks the park to refresh her spirit. Green notes of daffodils embrace her. The scent of liquid ultramarine wafts in the air from a clump of blue-throated hyacinths. She feels the comfort of their sensuous embrace.

She meditates, her breath stilled by being in nature. She concentrates on the in breath followed by the out breath, is aware of her chest rising and that slight pause before the inhalation, exhalation. The clay has a life-quality too: overworked it dies and doesn't respond to touch, becomes brittle and breaks. She, like the clay, must rest and recuperate.

****

Chapter Three

Freshly picked from the garden, Ella's evergreen stems, together with the brown bulbous vase, have been binned; expendable. As she exits the café, no footsteps follow her. The bus stop has been suspended. Typical! She strides to the next one, only two minutes to wait.

The card reader pings green to her free bus card. Age does have certain benefits. She sits on the front seat and texts. Predictive text makes gobbledegook of certain words. Her breaths are sharp, sobs, intermittent. The rhythm of the bus, the familiar journey, allows her to edit the text and press send. She gets off, covers the few hundred feet to the blue door, unlocks it, and is greeted by the dog. She lets her out the back.

Holly just sits in the winter sun but doesn't pee. Annoyed, she calls the dog inside, puts on her lead, collects a poo bag, leaves her rucksack in the kitchen and goes out. She picks sticks up on her way through the park then sits on a convenient bench. Making sure no other dogs are about, she lets Holly off the lead and the routine of chasing sticks begins. Spying two yappy dogs, she puts the lead back on. Holly might have chased those tiny dogs, snarling after them. Might even have rolled them over out of fear or anger, much as she felt Anneke had reacted to her when she'd asked earlier, 'Where's my vase? That was my vase, you knew that didn't you?'

'It's in the bin. In the bin.'

'Binned?'

Ella had gone to the bin and looked. It was right down at the bottom, chipped on the edge, otherwise intact. Too far down to recover. She'd have had to throw herself in the black corporation bin to retrieve it. It's only a vase, just a thing, she tells herself. She wouldn't be demeaned by fishing it out.

She went back into the café and managed to finish her soup, spooning in one mouthful after another. It felt strangely comforting. Patrick was embarrassed and his eyes avoided hers apart from a pleading glimpse of 'sorry' while serving customers as normal.

Ella couldn't help noticing that Anneke's hair was freshly washed, shiny. Sometimes it was unkempt and greasy.

She tried to mitigate the situation, 'Anneke, your hair's looking nice.'

Anneke remained silent and disappeared into the kitchen, out of sight. Ella remembers her stomach tightening, with a ripple of sobs backing up inside her. She took her coat and rucksack, went to the loo and allowed herself a few precious tears; emotions she'd controlled since that morning began to roll. Then she wiped her eyes, blew her nose, pulled the chain, half smiled into the mirror, washed her hands and left, managing to stutter, 'Bye.' The unuttered 'thank you' caught in her throat.

But now she is back in the park, remembering all that. She realises the yappy dogs are now out of sight and releases Holly from the lead, free to chase sticks again. Any immediate danger has past. She sits on the bench and makes a decision that will fix Patrick permanently on the page.

It's at this moment that Ella thinks she'll start to write the novella. At least Patrick the Piscean will be between the covers of a book, where she can take him to bed every night. Anneke's metaphorical binning of her is inspiring Ella. Her lips crease into a determined smile and her tears of hurt are temporarily staunched. The outlines are sharp and clear, not fragmented by Anneke's angry firework display.

She gets a text: 'I will call.' She texts back: 'I have stuff to do. When I'm alone I'll text you and you can phone.'

Later, sitting quietly on the bus, her childcare done and her daughter's evening meal prepared, she texts: 'Can I meet you in the café?'

'Sorry, not possible.'

So, she can't meet him face to face. Fortunately the bus is stopping near some gardens, so she gets off. She sits in the gardens, practices deep breathing and texts: 'Ok u can phone now.'

Her phone rings. She lets it ring for a bit.

'Hello?'

'I'm really sorry this happened, but I don't want an atmosphere like that in my café.'

'I was hurt. I tried to be respectful. I even commented on her hair, how good it was looking.'

'I noticed. Her behaviour was unforgiveable. I'm really sorry. It shouldn't happen to you of all people.'

'Whatever you do with Anneke is your business; it's nothing to do with me. I just need your things out of your room.'

'I understand. Just give me a couple of days. It must be distressing having some of my stuff about.'

'As you don't want to be here it makes sense,' she says aloud, but she's thinking, *it's a constant reminder of what was, and isn't*. Then she spews out those words, which arrive like predictive text when it automatically spells out a well-used phrase: 'I love you, unconditionally.' Ella is just able to stop adding, '…as a mother would a child.' But does she mean that? Is that why, deep down in her subconscious, she doesn't want to have sex with him even though she finds him physically attractive? Does that make sense? She puts her thoughts on hold.

'Please don't use the word love.'

'I love you in the true sense of the word as a friend with kindness and compassion. I would be shit scared to have sex with you.'

The truth seems easier to voice now she is expendable.

'Me too, but I'm really grateful for everything you've done. I wouldn't be here without you. There's a definite connection between us. There's no doubt of that. The relationship I have with you is special, completely different from the one I have with Anneke.'

'Thank you.' Automatically her gratitude and politeness resurface, relieved he's acknowledging how she's made a difference to his life.

Ella feels she can't tell Patrick that she misses the hugs morning and night, the companionship whilst he was staying at hers. He wasn't there every night, but the last few months have been very different from living on her own. The fact that she could touch his skin, massage him, feel safe and wanted. Relax him.

'I don't think you should come down to the café for a bit. I'll text you when it's safe.'

'Shall I text you?'

'No, I'll let you know. I'm sorry I have to go now. I have to collect Anneke's child from after-school club. I seem to be landed with a lot of childcare lately.'

Ella knows that Patrick's boundaries are blurred. He is now acting as substitute father to Anneke's child. Something he doesn't really want. He's admitted that. Yet he often babysits on the nights Anneke wants to earn extra money.

This morning, in Ella's daily ritual, she'd picked out the card *Kindness*.

'Thanks for phoning back. Take care.' Her concern re-emerges. Hurt on hold.

'You take care too. Bye, Ella.'

'Bye Patrick.'

Ella cradles the phone in her hand. How she wishes she could hold his hand or at least speak to him face to face. Yet she is able to ink him onto the paper. Not be compliant, saying it didn't matter when he said he wasn't coming to hers, texting how he was going back to visit Anneke who needed him, or seeing his ex-wife because she was troubled.

Later she looks out the poem she'd written for him when he'd asked, 'How do you think you'll feel when I leave?'

'Devastated!'

'I really hope not.'

Then she corrected herself, 'I'll cope. I always do.'

'That's the reason I won't be staying too long. I don't want to hurt you and I know you are extremely fond of me.'

Ella has, perhaps, prevented Patrick from drowning in despair. He had not drunk all the time he stayed at hers, apart from the last two nights. Patrick is alive. He's survived. She isn't able to change what happened to Tony.

Ella knows she isn't responsible for Tony's death. She didn't own it but, nevertheless, a feeling of guilt sometimes popped to the surface like a piece of driftwood bobbing on the sea. She'd not always been kind; sometimes her caring had broken like an overused elastic-band under too much pressure. She dismisses her thoughts of the past. *Just keep them there. Life is now.*

She re-reads her poem:

I'm responsible for my happiness

I am totally aware of that

but you never know how you

are going to react to a situation.

You text that you are not coming to mine,

looking after a friend who's not well,

Anneke and her son, where

you feel you are needed,

that's a good feeling to have.

Ask when I'm free, you'll cook me food

and we'll be able to talk.

I'm out four nights in a row this week.

I'd been looking forward to a night in

saved you a roast dinner.

I was upset and cried momentarily

over-reacted, I missed you.

Emotional, well it had been an emotional

weekend, a family friend walking into the sea

leaving a suicide note, his cleaner distraught,

He had joked with her about doing it three weeks before.

She never thought it would happen.

I sat with her the following morning,

after an hour of listening, she smiled,

she imagined his cap swirling on the water.

I said hopefully the cold had stopped

his heart, wouldn't have known a thing.

She said with hindsight she should have guessed,

he'd told her not to come in on Monday morning,

he was having his pots valued,

and kept asking her was she upset about this?

But of course she could come on Thursday

at any time. So unlike him, he was a late riser.

Tonight I don't want to be alone

I decide to visit a friend who is doing the music

for the revised version of my play.

She offers me a cup of tea,

my choice, rosehip, given to her by a friend

from Alaska of all places – calming.

I leave after a chat, walk to the race course

and watch the firework display,

am greeted by 'I'm still standing'

by Elton John, talk to a father and his toddler

who stand next to me by the race-track rail

until the display begins.

Explosions of glittery specks fan the sky

while the full moon watches.

Tentacles of glistening stars hang momentarily,

opening like exotic flower heads

shedding their hues. Swirling silver and golden

spirals sweep the sky, while others

fan the horizon, diamanté-edged.

Propelled rockets burst,

detonate, their splendour scattering the sky

with squiggles, geometric shapes

painting abstract patterns,

shooting globules of colour, reds, greens, blues,

oranges, purples amidst the silver and golden rain,

are absorbed into the night sky.

Another swooshing sound

sparks off swathes of pink balls skyward.

Kaleidoscopic images spread their brilliance

glowing pigments dazzle, surge, twist

as the final flickers fade into the darkness.

I walk down the hill alone. It's chilly.

Catch the bus home.

Nibble food.

The coal embers glow in the dust.

I'd lit the fire earlier in the day

so the place would be cosy,

and I am writing this for me – us.

I know you're not responsible for making me happy,

that's something I can do for myself,

and I did, I didn't mope

I got on with it, enjoyed my evening.

Now it's time for bed and rest

I send you a friendly hug,

Sharing my evening in writing.

Ella sought out compassion in a friend, found solace. The fireworks, like passion, shot momentary colours, lit the gloom. They left smoky curls, like a post-coital cigarette, redolent of spent desire, scorched earth.

****

Anxiety makes Ella keep pressing the key pads, producing unreadable words which she corrects as she breathes out. Familiar phrases thread their way into the writing, to counteract the loss of a discarded gift: her evergreen stems, their rounded, glazed container.

She takes a piece of prepared clay and rolls it, pressing it down to make a firm, circular base for her vessel. She ensures the base is even and curves her fingers round it. Not too thick or it's liable to crack, but solid. Ella smoothes both sides with her fingers using gentle but firm strokes. The structure can now evolve organically.

****

Chapter Four

She smells the blanket that has covered his body in bed and when she massaged him on the couch. A slight acridity, an earthiness mixed with lighter tones of cedar wood, sea salt, a hint of tobacco, his pheromones. It makes her tingle. She pictures him hugging her. She imagines herself burrowing into his jumper, allowing oxytocin to be released. All it takes is thirty seconds. She imagines him in her arms. She's curled against his sleeping form.

Ella takes the blanket up to bed with her, musing that both Tony and Patrick would like the title of her book, *Between the Covers*, an allusion to cricket. Tony found cricket a peaceful pastime to watch; bat on ball, the field placing that he learned by heart. She felt him relax as he watched, while she sat and scribbled, knitted or occasionally observed an exciting bit when sixes were scored or there was a possibility of winning in the last few overs. The smaller grounds were often in a beautiful setting. It was pleasant being in a convivial place and less raucous than football. Patrick enjoyed sport too. He found it a way to unwind, watching a game being played out. There was a rhythm in the bowlers' trajectory of the ball, the sound of the ball on willow, the stance, the banter at the wicket trying to put the batsmen off their stride. What was the technical term? Yes, the word sledging came into her mind and Tony saying, 'You nearly had me stumped'. She smiled.

Ella is pleased she's writing, even if it is from her imagination. She thinks about her friend, Josie who's not been sleeping for nearly a month, constantly waking up after just ten minutes. She takes some melatonin from Patrick's temporary bedroom. Although he is no longer at Ella's, most of his stuff is still there, a constant jabbing reminder. She got the pills for Patrick or, more truthfully, she asked her daughter to order them on the internet. She wasn't able to be his sleeping pill and he wouldn't go to the doctor, so she'd ordered the melatonin. He didn't bother to take them regularly. He took the occasional pill, but hadn't persevered to get his body clock into some kind of rhythm.

Patrick was embarrassed that she had bought him a load of Christmas presents, so in the end she gave him just one, left the others in the bag. One left over was a book on sleep, which would be perfect for Josie. She finds an empty pill jar for the melatonin tablets, collects the book and puts them both on the table downstairs so she will remember them in the morning.

Now this is done, she should be able to settle. She goes back to bed and snuggles the blanket around her. Since Patrick left she's turned the heating down, and hasn't left it on as long. He'd felt the cold but, although she'd lost weight, her chubbiness kept her warm.

He'd commented in the past, 'I dislike my mirror image; old, white-bearded, thin.' She loved the inner man, the pleasure when she touched his skin, soothing away sorrow.

She starts to shiver so she wraps his blanket tightly around her, pulls the duvet over her shoulders and burrows down in bed. Her trembling gradually stops and warmth seeps through her body. She inhales Patrick's pheromone molecules, the earthy comfort of a cuddle. Tears swell; she wipes her eyes and pictures him lying there asleep: his shaven head, the tonsure shinier than the rest. She envisages her fingers tracing his outlines; his unshaven face, grey-haired, not bristly, but soft; his eyes closed (but when open they're blue grey), those eyes that mesmerise. She can easily get lost, be dragged down into them. She imagines his mouth twitching into a beguiling smile, her hands feathering his calloused hands.

She remembers the joy of when he first French-kissed her. He'd had his fill of whisky. Their tongues explored, intertwined. They were fully clothed. The feel of his tongue delving and at other times caressing, and Patrick saying, 'That's tasty.' It makes her smile. It's only the whisky that made him do it and they didn't do it that often, French-kissing, so it sticks in her memory.

She'd written him a poem reminding him.

Whisky makes me your woman

unleashes your tongue

recalls love, loss –

delves in my mouth

forgetting our promise

just to be friends.

Whisky makes me your woman,

how much do you remember?

I've long gone

when you fall into a stupor

wake up with the lights still blazing.

I want to be held

curled in your arms

tempted to burrow,

but I'm sober

don't want to drink.

I tear myself away

we sit apart

talk

eyes connect.

Whisky makes me your woman.

Sober, your embrace is more fleeting,

less searching.

She remembers the time she lay fully clothed next to him on their first New Year's Eve, French-kissing.

It had only been for a short while. She recalls his groans, little squeals of delight. They were like presents that her body had rhythmically squeezed out of him. Like the joy a child feels from a teddy bear that growls when you press his stomach in a certain place. A few days later she was suffering with snot and a cough. He said later that evening, that he'd not been feeling well. She smiled, it served her right.

This New Year's Eve had been different. They were apart and she texted him. He felt totally uninvolved in the function he was running in the café. Ella didn't know what got into her head, but she started sexting on how she felt when she thought of him. He had texted back: 'Have a lovely evening.'

And then: 'I kiss your lips. Our mouths are open. I feel different textures with my tongue.'

'I delve deep into ur warm sweet mouth.'

'OMG my cock is getting erect. I'm pulling it down.'

'The fire's glowing. I can feel my cunt opening.'

'Sorry I need to...'

'Don't tell me.'

'It won't take a minute.'

By this time, she was really turned on, needs to come, wants to come. So, she visualises him. One knee bent, the other straighter, she squeezes, feels the warm wetness, visualises him unzipping. They are in a locked room, there is someone wanting to come in. It's probably his wife. They must do it there – now. There's urgency, desire that's opening her more and more. Her vagina is warm, wet. She can feel him pushing, wanting it as much as she does. The want is pulling. Pushing. She can feel the seed coming. It's bursting, pulsating inside her. She's catching her breath, her eyes glaze, stare. Their breaths are panting, gasping, stuttering, wanting every last drop; as she groans her mouth opens wide, screams, ululates in the relief. It's so sweet it's almost painful, that final reaching out and receiving. Both Ella and Patrick come together. He starts to text again: 'I'm on top of u pushing. The cum is coming. Ur panting.'

'It's come inside me, your spunk filling my cunt.'

Later he texted: 'The ultimate zipless fuck. I can't deny it, u really turned me on.'

She longs to be cradled in his arms. The warmth of being wanted, needed. She's reminded of when he talked about his sadness about mixing up sex, lust and desire, with love.

A vivid picture flashes into her mind, of a day, no an evening, in his old premises, the café bar, when they'd been canoodling – she liked that word – fully clothed, but enjoying the experience like a couple of prepubescent teenagers. Her expression must have changed. Well, it had. She wanted to stay the night, but she knew she must do the right thing and go home.

He was visibly concerned that her happiness had vanished like a cloud going over the sun, so he grabbed her from behind, his hands flirting with her. As they look at their reflection in a broken window their lips curled. He gently patted her arse, and Ella realised this was her cue to leave, which she did, managing to keep a fragile smile intact.

Ella grasps his blanket, nuzzles her head into it, as though Patrick is there and converses for them both. It's like a filmic scene and she is directing it.

As she cradles him in her arms, her legs are beginning to part. His hands and body move downwards, sensing… She rolls the blanket onto her belly then presses some of it between her legs. Her back arches and now Patrick is parting her legs with his hands, her knees splay outwards. His hands are holding her buttocks so her swollen belly can deliver.

She is commanding him with her pen so he cannot deny her, 'Open me; sweep me with your tongue'.

She imagines his tongue licking her cunt. She arches her head further back, grabs the bottom of his neck, which is rosier than the rest. Her fingers are pulling the skin up and down, stretching it, and simulating the movement of his tongue which is going deeper opening her even more. It's feasting, teasing, feeling the different textures as though she is a gorgeous ripe fruit. She is about to lose control.

The lens blurs out of focus. The pen stutters – it feels uneasy, wants to dance within him. This is safer. He's drunk, but she's quite sober. She allows her hips to shimmy, her arms to move to the beat. Their lips meet. They kiss. Their bodies rave to the music, twisting and turning. They dance with their hips side by side, gyrating. She is full of energy, full of joy.

He demands, as he presses against her, 'Can you feel it?'

Yes, it was hard, pushing against her, demanding attention like a gloved hand, or like metal wanting to penetrate, investigate how much she'd dilated.

His erection demands satisfaction, ink must be spilled. Her flesh cannot fight. It's soft and giving. In the shadows where past parallel lives exist, she hears the whispered words, 'It'll be fine if we do it standing up'.

She feels her skirt being scrunched up as her pants are ripped off. She fights trying to replay, get back to the music, but the moment of ecstasy has gone. He's gripping too tightly, stifling her breath, and she can't squirm out. She feels the instrument carving its way in.

'This is what you get, you prick teaser.'

She's no longer in control. The pen has been usurped.

Her body goes limp, but the perpetrator takes over her pen, pushing until she hears his elongated moan. She feels his release, the ink spills, leaves a blotch on the paper. She's discarded like a wrung-out rag. She washes her body, the seeped blood; she scrubs and removes any traces from her memory. Her skin is raw. Scum has temporarily stained the bath, she removes the crime.

In her mind it's many months later, when she hasn't come on, and Ella realises that her belly is swollen and a seed has taken root. She can no longer deny the growth. She can feel it's alive. A life cuckolded inside her. She fantasises that's how Patrick's mum conceived him.

She swallows hard, sweat is pouring from her; she's still reeling in her imagination. Her belly is beginning to harden, so now she can go with the contraction and expel the foetus. She closes her eyes and with all her energy she pushes as a primal scream fills her lungs with guttural shuddering sounds. The baby's head has pushed down her birth canal, is crowned. Not long. He's on his way.

She hears Patrick's voice echoing in her head, 'I can't cope with rejection.' She knows as she pants between contractions, how she must push this conception through the moist pulsating darkness. Allow him to escape, breathe, to live.

She has given birth to Patrick. He's is no longer an invasive growth. He's a baby in Ella's arms, lying on her belly. Her breasts are tingling. Ella teases Patrick's mouth open with her finger and places it over her erect nipple, making sure he's latched on.

'Suck my darling, suckle the sweet milk.' She knows Patrick craves unconditional love, sweetness in his life. This is why he yearns for alcohol; alcohol, full of sugar, that allows him to forget and dull the pain. He longs to be loved and so he tries to... how to express it... he gets sucked into helping people, tries to please their needs, and needs above all to be needed.

Ella mutters as she comforts him, 'Come to me Patrick. Your mother loves you. She didn't mean to hurt you.'

The afterbirth slivers, no, snakes out of her. Just like the phrases in her novella push themselves into her awareness, allowing Ella to birth herself into being.

When she later reminisces, she sees how Patrick has given her back a connection to her physicality; 'the animal in all of us,' is what he called it. She and Tony decided not to have children yet, occasionally, when she has felt an orgasm, Ella's imagined giving birth to their child. She'd contained an inner longing even though her rational mind barred the possibility. Ella, who from childhood until the present accepted constraint, was as acceptable as school uniform, emotion neatly hidden by a fixed and acceptable appearance, is trying to loosen the cocoon that swaddles her.

Sleep, which often evades her, now embraces her. Her tousled hair sinks into the pillow, her limbs curl into the foetal position, and exhaustion engulfs her.

****

Ella teases the letters off the page – rewrites them in her head where she can let them fly in her imagination, manipulate them. It's time to take more clay, to make the coils. Slowly she rolls them between her hands, equalising the pressure so the coils are of similar dimensions. The coils will curve round the base and make the bowl's belly.

Ella's passion is like a bulb, hidden in the dark moist earth, that gives birth to Patrick, gives him life. She weaves an umbilical cord, linking her conscious to her subconscious mind. This is Ella's strong connection to earth, her physicality and her desire to nurture him.

****

Chapter Five

Ella manages to sleep and now night has broken into day. Calmly she does her morning routine; her stretches, sends healing to Patrick, his family, her friends and family, and she requests of the universe that she may find love. Well she has, hasn't she?' But not with someone that can reciprocate, be with her for any length of time.

Yet she knows this experience has opened her to understanding that she too has wants, can feel lonely. She is grateful to her family and friends for their support. She looks at a thought for the day from her *Little Book of Wisdom* from the Dalai Lama. Love and compassion are the ultimate source of human happiness and our need for them lies at the very core of our being. A good mind, a good heart, and warm feelings – these are the most important things.

The card for the day she picks is *Peace*. From the healing angel cards she picks *Positive Expectations*.

It's funny the things she misses: the chirping of his phone alarm, then going up the stairs to give his bedroom door a knock, making sure he's got up. She loves hearing his voice, it's genial, kind. Whereas her limbs are stiff in the morning when she's on her own, when he was staying with her the stairs presented no difficulty. She guesses the released endorphins helped.

Ella remembers Patrick texting, asking if, hypothetically, could he move in with her just for short time as he knew he was drinking too much. He wanted to be somewhere safe and comfortable. She can play the scene back it is so vividly etched on her mind, like a photograph in an album. They are sitting in her small, comfortable living room.

'Why don't you look into my eyes? Sometimes I feel I'm not here.'

Ella wishes he wasn't staring at her and she could revert to her pen. Eyes in the past have always criticised, queried. She loves him being at hers, but how can she tell him his eyes suck her inside him? Now water and earth are indivisible, fossilised as one.

She mutters, 'I'll try, but it's difficult.'

She can't tell him the connection seems so strong that she disappears. She's afraid and excited. She wills herself to try and look directly at him. It happens again and for that split second she can almost feel her body being gulped into those grey blue eyes. She lets out a sigh.

'What's wrong?'

'Nothing,' she stutters.' She's never lied to him.

'Please, I want to understand.'

'Understand what, something I can't even explain. It's just...'

'Just what exactly?'

'It feels as though I'm being interrogated.' She doesn't want him to dismiss her as a mad emotional woman.

'I am interested.'

'Well, you'll think I'm barmy – laugh.'

'Try me. I promise I won't laugh.'

'If I look at your eyes I get this funny feeling as though...'

'I'm listening.'

'As though they are gulping me down, yes that's it. They are gulping me down, swallowing me whole.'

He smiles, laughs.

'I said you would find it amusing.' She turns her head away.

'Sorry, please go on.'

'I think we have some deep connection.' She can't say 'spiritual', 'soul connection' or that she feels they were destined to meet.

'I don't doubt that.'

'Thank you, but it's more than that.'

'Please explain.'

How could she say that in a former life they could have known each other?

'You'll think me stupid.'

'Not at all. You are a very observant, sensible person.'

Ella realises she needs to be in control, so she changes the subject; and she knows Patrick is tired, needs to relax. She could give him a massage. Something they both enjoy.

'You're tired. I can tell. Let's just go to bed.'

'You know I'm not ready for a relationship.'

'Yes, I realise that and what you are saying is that we have to be good.' She doesn't know what made her say this. Maybe it's because he likes a play on words. 'And I am good.'

She giggles inwardly. Can you giggle inwardly? It makes her feel cheeky, flirty.

'I don't doubt that.'

He's smiling, not angry.

'Well at least let me give you a massage, just your neck, back, shoulders.'

'But you're tired too.'

'I enjoy it and you'll relax and hopefully sleep, and it relaxes me too.'

In this way she gets to touch him, feel his skin, be intimate, caress him, and not feel rejected. Her fingers can heal, say all the things her mouth fails to express.

'Well are you going to be a man or not?'

Patrick leans back in the chair.

'Take your shirt off and then I can do it properly.'

She bends over him and undoes a couple of his shirt buttons, then places her hands on his neck.

'I give in.'

He pulls off his shirt.

She kisses his head.

'Thank you.'

'That's better, now just relax and enjoy.'

Ella massages him very gently. She can tell by his breaths how he's calm, relaxed. Her fingers relish his skin, no – relish is the wrong word, linger on his flesh so they become as one. Her hands enjoy the elasticity of his skin.

The lens will not capture it all. The essence of when she holds him at the end of the massage. She is reluctant to unleash her grip, would cradle him softly to fill that gaping hole and let him slumber. Equally, he does want to come back into the room, but prefers to be held safe, protected in quietude. It is more serene than love-making. It's beautiful to be held, caressed. He cuddles her and they both go to their rooms.

'Sleep well, Ella.'

'You too darling.'

He's gone and Ella's on her own, yet she allows her thoughts to flicker back to Patrick the Piscean. Yet again she wants to feel the flow of water over her like a shower, warm and comforting.

She remembers him sat there on the other side of the table admitting he was really shy and after a pause he blushed, saying, 'I admit I had a very strict upbringing. I literally believed that if I masturbated I would go blind and felt very guilty when I did.'

They'd both laughed. She remembered she'd giggled, no snorted – uncontrollably; it wasn't particularly funny yet it tickled her. His expression was bemused before he confessed, 'I've never been very good at the sex bit. It would be a disappointment.'

She wondered, was it excessive drink or maybe premature ejaculation? And Ella went on to admit sex hadn't been amazing for her either, most of the time.

'Well, when I was really turned on with Tony, and actually enjoying sex, he would turn around and say I was like a daemon, or rather daemoness, which didn't help my self-esteem.'

'But you're all woman, please believe me.'

They'd laughed nervously and she'd embraced his shoulders momentarily and let go, but not before skimming a kiss on his head. She realised he was tired, and they'd gone to their separate rooms. Patrick didn't sleep well, but she had put patchouli and frankincense on his pillow, resonating with the heavy notes of whisky, which would allow his body to go into a stupor and relax.

On another occasion when she asked why he liked her he'd said, 'Because you care, I feel safe with you, and because you let me go to bed when I want.'

Ella remembers Patrick telling her that his wife had accused him of being boring and going to bed early. She put it down to depression.

Tony hadn't slept well either. He had found peace in the end, but often sleep evaded him and only a convulsion would allow his body that relaxation it needed to unwind and fall unconscious.

Both Patrick and Ella have admitted being turned on by the massage and, in the privacy of their separate rooms, pleasuring themselves. Passionate feelings sweep over her like a clashing wave filling her with exuberance and joy. She wants to feel his ejaculate on her skin yet she also wants to be free of the ache.

If she spills it out onto the pages, maybe reason will turn off this emotion. What had drawn her to him?

Ella has given Patrick this poem. She remembers finding a copy in his room. She often gave him her writing to read when he went to bed, a bedtime story. She didn't include the poems when she packed up his things. She found he often used them to write his shopping lists on the back.

Pomegranate

The skin leathery, bruised red

blemished, yet pierced with

a knife vermillion juice

spurts from cut pith

hiding seeded rubies,

their taste bittersweet.

Lost souls find refuge

in the swollen womb-fruit,

protected till reborn

feeding the heart

with crimson nectar.

The incision allows

juice to ooze,

releases pent up passion,

remembering the monthly flow long gone.

Breathing, holding on till

the crescendo of wanting

gasps, stutters breath.

The feel of tongues delving,

exploring deep within,

rejoicing as the explosion of seeds

squeezes rhythmically between membranes

letting that frustration

secreted, locked within, dissipate.

She pleasures herself

imagining him with her

holding her hand,

forgetting being used

or her coming being

regarded as daemonic.

After looking at the poem, she remembers, he'd particularly appreciated the membranes, juice and being a voyeur of her pleasuring herself.

She takes a deep breath, focuses, and removes the two free expressive paintings that she hung up in his room earlier that week, anticipating his return – he's not coming back, yet his stuff is as he left it – an untidy mess.

One is of vibrant orange daffodils with clusters of brush strokes and swirled lines that she'd washed over with a brush soaked in water, like shed tears. She had written: *death, life, imprint, decline, decay, shadow, shore, shell, reverberate, sing, tap, love you Dad, dread, despair, laugh.* These words had rolled out of her brain and transferred themselves through the loaded paintbrush swirling onto the work. On the next piece of sugar paper she'd painted daffodils standing tall, as did her mother's in the vase next to her when she died. And she'd inscribed the words: *onward, soul, free, knowing the unknown, words do not fail, peace.*

Ella decides to take the two paintings and the remaining healthy snack bars from his table. She has breakfast, takes her vitamins and the remaining coconut water from the fridge, grabs the melatonin and book for Josie and puts them in her rucksack. She will have just enough time before yoga class to see Patrick. She puts her brightly coloured patchwork Macintosh on as it is raining.

As luck would have it, the bus is just coming, when she gets to the stop. She writes a note in her gratitude book, appreciating the bus's serendipitous arrival. She also writes that those recent fleeting moments of hope, love and friendship have been enough to spark the realisation that she can be loved for herself alone. Tears run down her face together with a half-smile. She relaxes her shoulders, looks straight ahead.

She walks down the road in her Elmer coat – Patrick called it that when she first wore it. His son had won a competition when he was little and the author of Elmer the Elephant had given him a signed illustration as a prize. It was still drizzling when she saw him going to the bins.

'How are you feeling?'

He said, 'Like shit.'

'I just want to thank you for yesterday.'

'For what?'

'For witnessing my pain and not trying to stop me crying. It made me feel better.'

'I really don't understand people.'

Patrick is amazed. Today they're holding hands. Well she's proffered hers and he's held out his so they swing the black bag together towards the bin. They've never held hands in public before. He notices she's happier.

'Are you just passing?'

She nods and takes out the coconut water to rehydrate him and the two pictures she's painted for his dad.

Patrick puts his arms around her, holds her close, but not too tight, and kisses her head.

'Your hair smells of coconut,' he comments.

She loves his sensuousness. It's like when he smells a pineapple, putting it right up to his nostrils breathing in deeply so he can judge, before he incises it with the blade, if it's overripe, fermenting, just on the edge or ready to be savoured, when the sweetness and acidity are in perfect balance. Ella loves sitting in her garden inhaling the fragrance of mock orange blossom, its honeyed sweetness.

She feels happy that crying has allowed a transformation to take place. Spontaneously she says, 'You will always be in my heart,' pointing to her chest, 'safe in there.'

He points to his heart and says, 'In mine too.' A tiny capillary of acknowledgement as tenuous as a spider's silken strand, but it nourishes her. She feels truly blessed that the tears have cleared a blockage of resentment. The friendship will not be severed.

She goes to see her friend Josie with the melatonin and book.

'How sweet of you to remember.'

Try not to switch the light on every time you wake up, and have a banana by your bed to eat when you wake. Take the melatonin half an hour before you want to sleep.'

'Thanks again. You're an angel.'

Ella goes to yoga, part of her structure for the week.

****

Ella is trying to weave routine activities within reminiscences of loss. She works instinctively. She decides to wild journal. Tears up a piece of paper strewn with words, ripping them apart, sticks them onto card, covers them with acrylic paint and ink. Playing, she lets her inner child explore, creates organically, enjoys the texture, colour, movement of hues that flow onto the paper. She loves this freedom to play, to just be Ella rather than being defined by a structure.

Ella makes sure that the first clay coil is securely fixed to the root of the structure, so the vessel will be strong – not collapse. She then smoothes the bottom of the coil into the base so it becomes invisible, grows into the structure. She neatly snakes coils on top of the outer edge of the previous loop so each one is slightly longer. Organically the form expands outwards, like her heart opening.

****

Chapter Six

She remembers the telephone conversation after his dad died. He was coming back that day. He called her 'Sweetie', not his normal way of addressing her.

She immediately asked, 'Are you coming back to mine?'

'No I won't be. I can't have three people in love with me. I've only ever wanted friendship from you.'

'Really?'

This is all she wanted too. But she tested the boundaries, needed to know she was desirable, and exposed her passionate nature. Why with him? Ella was always so self-reliant and had got used to being on her own.

Patrick apologised, 'It was my fault. I'm to blame.'

'No, I apologise it was my fault,' she replied. 'I know I shouldn't have pushed and pulled. We need to talk face to face.'

She'd meant to say this ages ago but there never seemed an appropriate time and, let's face it, she liked the flirtation, imagining

Patrick as lover, friend, companion. It was comforting like a child's cuddle blanket. It made her feel secure.

'We will talk,' he promises.

But, as normal, the time is postponed which increases her distress. He's always warned her he wouldn't stay long, knowing, she is so fond of him. He doesn't want to hurt her. She decides she will not confront him, until after his dad's funeral.

Ella needs to focus, do something practical. She has woken up very early. If she stays in bed she'll just start to want him, get tearful. The excess ice in the freezer has been annoying her for ages. So today she tackles it with bowls of hot water. Initially the frozen blocks refuse to budge, like her heart locked into coping strategy, not even daring to acknowledge there is anything missing. Her teenage attraction to Patrick aroused her hormones and feelings she'd long dismissed as irresponsible.

Multi-tasking, she starts to simmer the frozen redcurrants, a gift from a friend, with left over foraged blackberries. She takes apples from the fruit bowl, peels and chops them, adding them to the mixture. The ice begins to melt and her tears flow. Flowing like the excess water on the floor. Ella collects the icy chunks, makes sure every surface is clean and dry, and puts the freezer stuff back in place. It's no longer littering the kitchen surfaces. She sieves the pulp so the jelly's not full of pips.

Momentarily her eyes start to fill up again. She must concentrate. She adds sugar, stirs the mixture allowing it to simmer, then boils it vigorously until the settling, no – she means until the *setting* point is reached. She bottles the deep crimson jam. Some spills onto Ella's hand like menstrual flow, hers dried up decades ago. Her gut aches once again. She remembers the time her period was late and she thought she might have been carrying Tony's child. Her period was particularly heavy, maybe an early miscarriage, but more likely caused by the coil, her chosen form of contraception. Tears begin to stream down her face.

She blows her nose on toilet tissue, showers, gets dressed, eats breakfast and does her morning exercises. She does the washing, cleans, tidies, wants to hear his voice, feel his arms around her but knows it's not possible. She has no right to make demands. She must be sensible. Always responsible, do what is expected.

She has shed more tears in these last few days than she has for years, allowing those bottled emotions to be free. She's glad he's opened her to love once more. Did she tell him that she eats a whole bar of nut chocolate instead of having a hug from him? It was certainly more fattening, but nonetheless good. Fuck, it's good that she's cleaned the freezer and tidied. Now's there's the rest of the list to tackle: shopping, delivering cards, presents.

The painting course is a creative diversion, something just for her. She's allowed treats. Ella arrives a little late and the group are discussing Goethe and how he felt that the whole of the life cycle of the plant should be taken into account. On the table are displays of lilies, tulips and daffodils, in varying states of bloom and decay. Ella finds she is the only one to choose the daffodils. She chooses daffodils as she remembers the green notes they splay out. They also last longer in the garden than tulips, which are more flamboyant but shorter lived. She dismisses lilies whose scent is sweet overpowering, cloying.

'Draw what you feel about the flower and its essence.'

Ella takes yellow and purple pastels; yellow for its healing, purple for spirituality. The daffodils' colour of buttery yellow, blasts gold out to the sky. Intuitively she had chosen purple, yellow's complementary colour.

'Now draw the flower, holding it in one hand and the pastel in the other, without looking at it.'

Ella grasps the stem firmly, draws without looking, in a burnt umber pastel. The likeness is a little abstract, but not unrecognisable.

The group has a break to look at their pictures. Everyone has their own style, all with different qualities; it shows their connectivity. Some of the tulip petals look like tail feathers. It prompts Ella's mind back to something she's just learned about a species of birds. Their co-operation is so natural it helps their survival. What the hell were they called? Yes, that's it, long-tailed tits. Never antagonistic, they travelled in flocks, family and friends flew together. Their nests were built from lichen, moss, feathers and cobwebs and expanded as their brood grew. During the cold they helped each other, huddled together. Didn't just keep to their own kind but included other species; great tits, blue tits, gold crests etc. Maybe that's why she loved Patrick; he welcomed everyone that entered his café and the Centre had that same feeling. She hears the facilitator of the group saying, 'Now paint a whole lot of flowers together. The last set task is to paint a trilogy: bud, full bloom, and then the withered flower.'

The one that most pleases her is the trilogy: the bud, which is partially covered with a greenish brown film; the full bright yellow trumpet; and then the withered petals painted in ochre, the petals dull, shrivelled, faded, like spent tobacco.

The two free paintings allow her imagination to express itself freely on the page. These are the pictures she gives to Patrick in memory of his dad. Ella likes the freedom to express herself just like when she wild journals. The group has been quiet and meditative, just what she needs.

Ella loves story telling. She made up stories for her children, now for her grandchildren, and bedtime reading for Patrick. Later today it's the monthly storytelling group that she attends regularly and helped start. She puts herself and Patrick into a mythical tale, knowing how stories heal and are therapeutic. This story is just for her and the group.

Aurora and Zelis

The bee was out flying in the late autumn and she sensed something amber and sweet in the air. Her name was Aurora and she had smelled the perfume in the distance, from a certain place, so she flew back to that exact same spot where she sensed the nectar and sure enough there was one male flower still remaining on the vine that clung precariously to the wall.

The vine was amazed when the bee declared that she wanted to begin her dance of love there. So, Aurora began to show the flower a few steps of her dance, ones that lay in her shadowy past and to her delight, as the memory of the steps returned, he embraced her. Yet something in her body reminded her that this was not the season, nor the place, for total revelation of each and every intricate step. There were indeed steps that they took together, but others she practised alone in the sanctity of her hive. The memory was painful yet pleasurable.

The vine flower would sometimes hide his face and she would go through a leafy maze or, later in the year, through the debris of withering leaves to envelope his drooping form. There was a sense of desperation, an abject sadness, yet when she discovered him hiding, there was also joy. She felt his sadness and wanted him to feel the vibrancy of her being. She still sensed it was not their time. The flower had imbibed the early morning dew and was drunk. The waft of rich amber nectar made him seek out the next steps in their dance. She enjoyed their movements. The hairs on her body prickled with excitement, but also apprehension. Yet she sensed he was distancing himself when he chided her gently, told her to behave herself. They sat apart.

She never knew his name so in her heart she called him Zelis. They grew fond of each other and she still visited, but tried not to linger as his petals and stamens began to tinge brown. They both knew the dance of love would never be completed. Yet in practising those steps Aurora had sensed youth, joy, in a body that she'd allowed the seasons to pass by unnoticed, apart from the occasional festival or dance.

She comforted and nurtured Zelis, as a mother would a child, yet the feeling she had within her was different. She learned at times, when he asked her to leave or purposefully retreated, that he needed to rediscover his inner being. He was neither hateful nor rejecting her but allowing the sadness he felt to be acknowledged, knowing it would pass. Aurora could make him laugh and dance for a while, but sometimes he needed to be alone to decide whether he would cling to the vine or totally let go.

Recalling the steps made her feel brave, rediscovering the blood coursing through her veins. Zelis would always be special in her life. His perfume was the key to allow her to rediscover the beauty of a dance, which her body would unleash in the spring when fresh flowers bloom, scenting the air.

Ella gets a text from Patrick after days of being away with his dying dad: 'Hi Ella, sorry to have been so silent. Things will work themselves out, trust me on this. I am away till tomorrow night. Will be in touch.

Sorry for any pain. It's undeserved and possibly something I could have mitigated better. You are a very special person to me. That will never change. X'

Ella remembers when Tony's dad was dying in a hospital room. Ella drove Tony to the hospital to join the family who sat in a side room. Tony looked at the clock, wrote a poem while waiting for his dad to die. She held his dad's hand, and got reprimanded; she was a daughter-in-law, not family. She sat quietly, hands in her lap. In the middle of this family goodbye, the cleaner came in to take the yellow contaminated bag away; bizarre. Her father-in-law eventually breathed his last breath; she left the room in tears. Ella dashed to a window where Tony's brother-in-law put an arm round her and she recalls him saying, 'You see there, that whitish-grey square building in the distance? That's where I went to school.'

'Where's the college Tony went to?'

'You see – right there, on the far right in the opposite direction, by that church spire.'

'And the swimming pool?'

'The swimming pool is over there, in the distance, nearer the sea.'

Ella reflects how the swimming pool is where she'd met Tony on their second date. Strange, because he didn't really like swimming but she loved the water. His body wasn't naturally buoyant. The conversation had brought some normality to the day.

Ella remembers Patrick telling her that when the district nurses came in to look after his dad, this also brought him normality about being with his parents. He was able to cook, do errands, talk to the medical staff, felt lighter. Towards the end, 'a void of darkness swallowed him whole.' Those were his words, if she remembered rightly. He then sank into gloom and depression. She imagines Patrick stifling his tears with drink. One of the carers couldn't move his dad as she had a bad back. There had been many more frustrations.

A few days later Patrick texted: 'Dad's died'.

Patrick was dealing with loose ends, trying to find the threads to cover his despair, sometimes matched with disbelief that his dad had now gone. He was doing the necessary things to move on when the balance of his life altered. His dad's body gave out, his mind dilapidated, he became a shell of the erudite man and great sportsman that he once was, but he recognised Patrick to the end.

Ella takes a breath and tells herself it's not weak to cry and thinks back to Patrick letting himself into her house. She recalls the conversation.

'I don't think you understand what I'm going through?'

Ella said, 'I can't rescue you, save you, but I can listen.'

'Did I mention you bloody rescuing me? I will just get into a car, drive too fast into a lorry, and it'll be done.'

'Don't even think it or, for that matter, say it.'

'I wouldn't do it. It would upset too many people.'

Ella thought, *Well why threaten to do it? Are you thinking of me at all?*

'I just want to get away, let there be an end. I really don't think you can understand what I'm going through.'

'I understand only too well. I don't need that shit, Patrick. Don't need someone who will re-dig into fallowed scars.' Were they fallowed, has she really laid them to rest? Well, she's tried. Tony's ashes in the garden were covered with vegetation, grape hyacinths, forget-me-nots to bloom in spring, summer.

'Don't be so melodramatic,' Patrick told her.

Ella said, 'I have to tell you this. I have to make it clear – I don't want this to happen again.' She didn't want to make it possible for him to hurt her again.

'I didn't know where to go, but I came back here because I feel safe and I trust you.'

'I realise you are drunk, quite bloody drunk, but I'm glad you felt you could come back to mine.'

He sits down in the chair.

'I know you're upset Patrick, but why don't you tell me what's bothering you?'

'It's just Christmas was so awful. It was the only time Dad didn't recognise me. He wouldn't eat or drink and I really thought he would die.'

He began to sob. She held him gently, allowing his emotions to release. Whispered, 'You know you can tell me anything. You can let go, I don't mind.'

She thought, *Just let your emotions out – don't cover them up and drink yourself into a stupor.*

Now she is on her own again, Ella wishes that she could hold Patrick, be held by him, be embraced, feel safe.

She thinks back to the last time she saw Tony. She gave him his favourite food of beef stew and vegetables and a jacket to wear as he was shivering. He gave her a Christmas present, but then took it back. Ella gave him some photocopied poems with paintings to go with them. He mentioned going away with her to Turkey or Morocco for Christmas but she told him it wasn't possible.

He was grinning as he waved goodbye.

This was the last time she was to see him.

She recalls Patrick, that same night, being at home with her after he'd cried and kissing her repeatedly on the lips.

'I love you.'

She kissed him back.

He was really affectionate. Was this the result of the disinhibition of drink? She relished the affection, like a plant being watered after a long drought. Was it gratitude? Did he want to please her? She didn't know. Maybe it was in *vino veritas*? This was the only night that Ella followed him into his room.

They kissed on the lips, were giggly like teenagers. Patrick says, 'The older one of us should know when to leave.'

Even when drunk he's protective. They are gentle with one another. She kissed him for a final time, closed his door and went to bed.

She knew it was the drink. He wanted to please her. It wasn't for real, yet she desperately wanted to believe it was. In the morning, Patrick was quiet and berated himself. He could hardly hold his head up.

'I'm sorry for being such a plonker.'

She was angry. Was she really angry? He'd been stupid in upsetting her, but it was a defensive phrase, a reflex action, that statement – that she was incapable of understanding what he was going through. It was embedded in his psyche and exacerbated by drink. After the outburst he'd shown her affection, hadn't he? Her body ached to be hugged but Ella was quiet and compassionate, saying, 'I know that you have the ability to make people happy, care, make them feel special and that's a rare gift.'

Later he texted her: 'Ella, thanks for being so kind and understanding after my stupidity last night.'

****

Ella starts smoothing out the lines between the coils on the outside of the bowl so the loss will become bearable and the joins will be concealed. Her thumb strokes the coils on the outside of the container with a gentle but firm downward action. She is trying to meld her need for connection, knowing this attraction was more than just physical. She's disguising the boundaries now they're apart, masking her hurt. Her fingers enjoy the feel of particles smothering the cracked lines. It's soothing, smoothing and removing the indentations. It reminds her to be kind to herself. The action allows anger to dissipate. Compassion, touch are what's important.

She transforms her feelings into a story within her story. It's easier to accept them as a metaphor. The paintings illustrate her belief that death is not the end – it's an onward path.

Now Patrick has held death close too. The connection is stronger, will survive.

****

Chapter Seven

Patrick and Anneke like a drink and dabble with drugs. Well, Patrick took cannabis to sleep and has enjoyed a drink most of his adult life. Occasionally he abstains from drinking when it affects his capacity to work properly. His adoptive parents drank, the only parents he's known, so drink was an everyday occurrence. Ella doesn't care for drink but Patrick is like a drug; she can't get him out of her mind. He enables her to be her true self and safe at the same time.

She remembers the voice he uses when she gets a good word in Scrabble. He speaks in the same tone when praising Anneke in the kitchen, something he does frequently. Basically, he is kind and gentle. Ella remembers Patrick telling her that he believes Anneke feels an outsider and her command of the English language lacks understanding of innuendo, irony. Anneke, however, knows how to manipulate a man, make him feel needed.

Ella remembers seeing her in the kitchen while visiting the café – just a tiny moment but one of many.

'Patrick can you please help me?' She was trying to separate the ends of a black plastic bag.

He turned around, by which time her wet fingers had separated the two pieces.

'Oh, it's okay. I have done it.'

Patrick brings Ella her soup, serving it with a flourish. 'Would you like a sprinkling of parmesan on top of that?'

'Yes please.'

'Enjoy.'

Ella remembers, in the distant past, him laughing in the old café bar, saying, 'I wish you were my mother.'

She slaps him on the arm and retorts, 'Hardly, I would have been fourteen when I had you.'

They'd laughed.

But looking back, maybe this is what he really wants, a mother who really loves him, not one that rejected him at birth but a mother who gives him unconditional love. Is that why, in her fantasy, she'd given birth to him and cradled him in her arms? Ella wanted to heal the hurt, which she knew she could never do. It just bled onto the page and she'd tried to scrub it out. Perhaps she was as controlling as his adoptive mother. The thought was too painful, she didn't want to go there.

Ella remembers that, when they'd first met, he had been concerned about his parents, but initially more about his mum. He had to leave the business as his mum had to go into hospital for heart investigations. His dad had dementia but was being cared for. His mum survived the operation but she was still trying to be in control and wanting to look after her husband.

She remembers Patrick discussing his mum. 'My mother ended up feeling unwanted, alienated, sitting in a freezing ante-room refusing to move, not taking her pills, having lurid hallucinations which later she admits she might have dreamt.'

'Maybe they were little T.I.A.'s, mini-strokes?'

'Could well be.'

He continued, 'Now she won't let me investigate the boiler bill. It's two and half thousand pounds. I just want to make sure she's not being ripped off. There's no breakdown of labour and parts.'

'I can understand you get frustrated.'

'Frustrated is not the word. The other weekend she was going on about spoons.'

'Why about spoons?'

'Just because the carer isn't English and doesn't distinguish the difference between a teaspoon, a soup spoon, a desert spoon, my mother gets beside herself. It's still a bloody spoon!'

'Your mother has lost the control that made her feel safe. It's annoying but understandable.'

'I feel she married Dad to get herself out of her situation of sharing a house with other girls after her parents died.'

Ella knew Patrick was very fond of both parents but always found his dad easier. At this moment his sympathies were with Dad as he was annoyed with his mum for being so bossy. He hated rules, being told what to do. Ella found her mum easier to relate to and yet her dad had probably been kinder but, nonetheless, critical of her relationships.

Her dad wanted her to be something she wasn't; a teacher. She was, however, a very good teaching assistant. Dad would insist on introducing her as a teacher. Did a job define who you were? She did take on that role in the special school when the real teacher had time out, but that was different. Yes, maybe she liked to take control of a situation too. Her thoughts were interrupted by Patrick, 'I think my dad needs more stimulation, needs to go out and see a show.'

'But what will happen to your mum?'

'Well Dad's not very nice to her, I admit that. He says she's a very bad secretary and he'll be getting a new one soon to replace her.'

'It's the dementia, they often get very angry.'

'She needs to go into hospital or a care home and get some real rest.'

Ella is hesitant, I've written something for your mum. My step mum had Alzheimer's so I understand. Shall I read it to you?'

'I'll read it later.'

Ella enjoys writing poetry and she knows he is concerned about his parents, especially his father's dementia, so she's written him a poem mirroring Patrick's dilemma in maintaining equilibrium with his parents.

To Mum

Mum if I could gather all the

ravaged leaves

and build a canopy of love,

I would.

But I can only

whisper words of comfort

through the phone.

Dad's mind like

autumn winds is swept away,

his neurones stripped bare.

It's not that he doesn't care

he can no longer piece together

the puzzle of your lives.

It makes your heart ache,

and mine too,

that you must witness

this unfamiliar dance where

everything you once held dear

is strewn on the ground.

I'm lost for words of comfort

where Alzheimer's dementia

shreds your temper

causes you so much pain.

I wish I could cup the hurt

stop the tide with a hug

but I know the debris shatters

your wellbeing.

Deep down in your soul

Dad did and somehow does

feel for you but is lost,

confused, clutching to find reason.

Connectivity

is starved of oxygen.

Frustrated he seeks

to gain some equilibrium

by building something anew,

and harms the one he loves.

It's the disease, illness

that's out of control.

I send my love and hope

that there are times when

your heart stills and you know

you are cherished, hugged, loved.

Take time to rest,

look after yourself.

Let go the anguish

and know you have done

nothing wrong, only reacted

to what seems so untrue

and stirs up hatred,

confusion in you.

Let your focus soften,

accept, acknowledge it's beyond

your power to control Dad's thoughts.

They're irrevocably damaged

no one's fault.

Limit the harm,

I know it's difficult

but breathe the anger out,

let peace settle

like sunrays through clouds.

I will always love you both

in different ways.

Several days later Patrick said, 'That poem was beautiful. I was tempted to send it to my mum.'

'Why didn't you?'

'Because she would realise it wasn't mine and would be upset I'd shared my thoughts with someone who she doesn't know.'

'Well, I'm glad you liked it.'

'Dad is still being beastly to her and threatening to replace her with someone better.'

'She must feel very isolated.'

Patrick just nodded and poured himself a large whisky. 'Do you want anything?'

'A pandalicious please.'

Patrick had introduced her to the flavour, a mixture of liquorice and chamomile. It was good for the digestion and she liked the unusual taste. As a child she loved Pontefract cakes; black, slightly chewy, a texture between toffee and fudge.

'Coming up.'

'You know you said about your mum being isolated? It reminds me of my friend.

Guess what? I've got a poem, I wrote for her. It's here in my bag.' She'd read it on local radio that day and she didn't give him time to refuse, but launched in.

Sundays are tinged with shadows,

memories of Mother leaving us

after family lunch prepared with love.

Duty bound she goes to visit her mother,

who's sick in the mind,

to return to the family that evening

or, if not, her absence lingered

to early Monday morning.

My father could not fill the void,

he lacked the painterly skills

to sustain the rays of warmth,

comforting tones.

Like the ink blot's dark stain that

spills onto canvas,

it's difficult to erase.

That was long ago, but Sunday

afternoons are still tarnished with

sadness, a void, regrets,

but unexpectedly you're at the door

coming to share

your happy event I could not attend.

Momentarily the heaviness lifts

and the well of absence shifts,

you are here in the present, sharing.

She allowed a slight pause. 'That's the end. It wasn't too long was it?'

'You're very talented you can feel that emptiness.'

'Thanks.'

Here's your tea. You know I remember Dad and Mum taking me on the autobahn.'

'So you were in Germany?'

'Yes, they were taking me to boarding school and I remember the car stopping outside the school. They arrived later than expected. My father was ashen and my mother hysterical. I was trying to hang onto the car door but my hands were ripped away and I was carted through the front door.'

'My God, that must have been horrible.'

Ella went over to him and was about to embrace him, take her hands in his. She stopped herself.

'It was like being in prison. I still smell the fear, loathing, the reek of sweaty boys. It's lodged in my nostrils. I was there for four or maybe five years. The dread that filled my body when I had to go back each term still regurgitates inside me.'

She put her arms round him, 'God, how awful.' Such inadequate words for being put away, locked away.

'It was a long time ago.' She felt his body stiffen and let go. She felt he wanted to dismiss the subject. She would have been better being silent and yet she continued, 'But not something you've forgotten.' What a banal remark to make. Patrick is looking down.

She notices that very rarely does he allow her to take his hands in hers; he will gently move them away. His hands that were torn from the car door, now calloused.

Ella sat opposite him. She's reminded of Tony's experience at public school and says, 'Tony, my late husband, hated public school and was probably molested by older boys, bullied at least. In his last term he played hooky most of the time, but he left home on his bike and returned at the expected hour. He never admitted this to his parents until he was middle-aged.'

'So, they had no idea?'

'No, I don't think so. His father was furious because he'd been paying fees.'

'I bet.'

'Tony felt left out, alien; he was brainier than the boys in his age group, so his peers were all older and emotionally much more mature.'

'It must have been difficult.'

'He told me about the time when he was asked to find out if a certain girl was a virgin. The other boys watched as he went up to her and asked, "Can you tell me please, are you a virgin?" and got slapped round the face. The boys were hysterical with laughter.'

Patrick grins, 'He was very innocent.'

'Strangely, enough later in life she became a doctor's secretary and they became friends. Tony found relating to people difficult.'

'I can sympathise.'

'Yet he was desperate to please and, knowing his parents wanted him to receive a prize at the end of term, he wrote an essay on proving Kennedy's assassinator could not have been Oswald. They were very proud to see him walk to the podium and be congratulated.'

'Strangely enough, I want to make people happy too.'

Ella laughed, 'And you do.'

Ella's flibbertigibbet mind returns to discussing Patrick's mum facing the end of her husband's life.

'I know it's odd but what your mum wants to do by asking to learn how to manipulate the hospital bed is to be able to please your father, make him more comfortable. Do something practical for him.'

He retorted, 'It's the carer's job.'

'It makes her feel she is doing something helpful.' She blinked, shook her head, thinking of her own mum and said, 'You know when I was very little I really disappointed my mum. I promised not to open my Christmas stocking and I let her down. I can still picture her face.'

She thought of the promise she made to Helen, his helper, that she would always keep an eye on Patrick, while she was finding the other poem she'd read on the radio. It revealed how physically appealing Patrick was, that yearning to touch and feel him was so important to her, like a vital ingredient in a recipe; like nutmeg and knob of butter put on top of the tapioca pudding before it went into the oven. It made that gooey moreish skin. Ella had the urge to unwrap him, to see what made him behave the way he did. She found her poem and said, 'Just bear with me I'm just going to read you one more poem.'

The mother who lost out to the moon

The all-seeing moon

shone big and bright

illuminating a silhouette

of a stocking crammed

full of delicious

humps and bumps.

She squeezed her eyes

shut, clenched her fists

but temptation gleamed

her eyes open and the

moon was her conspirator.

She fondled the stocking

lying beside her

feeling every contour,

until fingers itched to

undo one tiny present –

not one more.

Teasing the paper from

the hidden secret she

wondered at the intricacy

of the pattern, such a

small cup the size of

a fingernail. What else

lurked in this lucky dip?

Fevered fingers raced through,

no longer careful but ripping

at lovingly concealed packages

to reveal a miniature

china tea service

which in amazement

she placed on her pillow.

Her face was aglow, but as

a cloud closed over the moon,

hurriedly items were rewrapped

and stuffed back into the stocking.

At the glint of day

a child's guilt was

seen in the hurt of her mother's face,

who had lost out to the moon,

whose eyes spied the wonder of discovery.

'I really like that.'

Ella looked at Patrick and realised his face looked drawn, maybe even fed up. 'Sorry I have been very self-indulgent reading my stuff; you must be bored stiff. I need to go. You need to rest.'

'You should keep on writing, get published properly. But yes, it's true, I should probably get some shut eye.'

'I'll be on my way.'

'Do you want a taxi?'

'I've got a bus card. It's fine.'

'Are you sure?'

'Of course. Take care, Patrick. Goodnight.'

'Thanks for popping in. Sleep well, Ella. See you soon.'

They hugged and Ella left.

She recalls having the weirdest of thoughts on the bus back home. She wants to re-gift him her virginity. Show him a mother's unconditional love. Be soft and gentle as she is in the massage, the way she can touches and relaxes him.

Ella is excited at the feelings within her yet also scared that the union would be a disaster, so to imagine it in her head is safer. Here is perfection, sex on the page, which turns them both on, releases their desire in a safe environment on clean sheets, between the covers of a book. A book she can take up to bed and read every night.

Ella imagines him suckling her breasts, being his Earth Mother, healing that sorrow of rejection, whether or not he wants to accept that his adoption or boarding school have made a difference to how he feels about himself.

Is there a connection to their souls in a former life? The physical attraction she feels is so real and yet the gut feeling is that fucking him would be wrong. Was she his mother, lover in another time? She had this intuitive feeling, but was that proof to others? Was he her healer? He made her feel different. Was Ella his guardian angel at times of sorrow? Patrick the Piscean and Ella Earth would always be connected in a glimpse of sunlight and in that mosaic on her garden wall of two fish swimming in opposite directions but in the same pool, seeking happiness.

Ella thought Patrick the Piscean would pour water over these juggled thoughts but they swirl around in her head and she needs to put them down on paper even if their patterns splay out like organic, floating marbled colours. She is convinced some unexplainable truth lies deep within them. Ella decides she will just leave them to drift in and out of a reader's mind and they will either be intrigued by the jetsam or disregard it as flimsy flotsam, flickering thoughts from an over-imaginative writer.

****

Ella takes up the bowl. Now she must smooth the inside so it matches the evenness of the outside. All trace of the coiled snakes will disappear. The dictionary defines cognitive dissonance as the experience of holding conflicting ideas, such as Ella being a mother, nurturing her inner child, and being aroused sexually; experiencing all these emotions, sometimes simultaneously.

Her thumb strokes the coils in an upward motion while she gently cups the bowl in her left hand. It is a delicate repetitive action; stroking the surface into line, dissolving the lumps and bumps, erasing loneliness, easing away sadness, just concentrating on the doing. The left hand twirls the bowl around as she works methodically, rhythmically. She holds the cup-shaped bowl and evens the top edge, holding it alternately in one hand and then the other, trying to gain some equanimity.

Happiness is fleeting but equanimity, contentment, is being in the moment and allows a momentum for life to flow rhythmically.

****

Chapter Eight

She remembers Patrick sitting on the other side of the table at her place, philosophising, 'What do you think about the dilemma of a man being able to pull a lever, changing the signals on a railway track to stop the train killing twenty people and, instead, only killing one? Or should the man who could pull the lever put himself in the path of the train to save everyone else.'

'That's a real conundrum, so many different things to take into account.'

'It's something that never fails to fascinate me. Working out the moral strategy. Is one solution more moral than another – is one life less precious than twenty?'

'Is it all about numbers? The commutations are endless.'

'How do you value a life? Surely every life is precious?'

'There are so many layers to think about and the reasons why people keep on going or decide...' Ella's voice sinks, slips off the page. The signal flashes red in her mind.

'What are you saying?'

'The man who was able to pull the lever might feel his life would be better used by saving a life or lives, like Tony who felt that perhaps he was able to give me my life back.'

Ella had found it difficult to press the keys down in those days but she knew Tony understood; sometimes it was all too much, but she didn't want to accept she was the reason. When she'd got her life back, the constant fear of what might happen lessened, but when Tony was alive and he had been late back, it increased... Had he had a seizure? Where was he?

Patrick just stays quiet and does not interrupt.

A pause follows like a piece of blank paper with possible words to be written on it. Words that wrangle, wanting to tell their truth, let it spill out. But in the end the statement that rises above the others is from Patrick.

'Sometimes I feel frightened for Anneke. Her mum died when she was very young, her brother died of a drug overdose and her husband hung himself. When she gets down, she sometimes says she doesn't realise why she should live?'

Ella instinctively stretches out to take his hand in hers, the anger and hurt she had felt towards Anneke easing from her body. Ella strokes his hand. Patrick feels close to Anneke, they have a bond, but what he has with Ella is different. She must accept that fact. Where mentally it makes sense, emotionally Ella finds it difficult.

Practising non-attachment, she realises she's not jealous. The unconditional love comes to the surface; that's why Patrick protects and respects her. Friendship doesn't tarnish, it endures.

She manages a smile, not a fixed grin, and a disparate thought comes into her head, yet holds some connection. She remembers telling him about Tony's quandary.

'Tony was fascinated about finding legal loopholes for tax avoidance, if that's the legal term, but on the other hand he was worried that this evasion would stop more schools and hospitals being built. His was a practical, mathematical mind that liked the challenge of working out a formula to help his client. It ended with the expediential solution, the altruistic and business mind conversing – discoursing with each other. Tony would always feel guilty because in saving the rich their taxes he was not serving the good of the population in general.'

'So, you mean he was torn between what was good for his client and society?'

'Yes, he had nightmares about it. It made him ill sometimes.'

'Surely society should come before the individual?'

'Yes, I believe it should.'

Ella gets up and goes into the kitchen. 'I'm just getting some water. Do you want anything?'

'Water's fine.'

They drink their water. Ella wants to feel close to Patrick.

'I think it's time for you to unwind, have a massage before bed.'

'Are you sure you're not too tired?'

'I would like to give you...' *one*, but before it slips out she says, 'a massage.'

'Who am I to refuse?'

'Just your back, shoulders and head.'

Patrick slips his jumper off.

Ella's hands sense naturally where more pressure is needed or where to linger and caress.

'You always hit the right spots.'

'My granny said I had healing hands. I used to put my hands on her shoulders when she had an angina attack. She didn't have to put a pill under her tongue.'

'Even from a young age?'

'I didn't question it; I thought all grandchildren had the gift.'

Ella wishes her mouth, her tongue, were as articulate as her hands, which know how to cherish the feel of Patrick's skin. She can feel his breath easing. He's relaxing as she teases the skin in her fingers, feels the delightful physical sensation. Ella presses his flesh more vigorously (a bad pastry maker, but a good bread maker), pummelling, pulling, stretching and easing it back in place. She chuckles to herself and remembers the children and her making bread, letting it rise, putting their initials on the bread rolls.

'What are you giggling about?'

'Oh, I was remembering me and the kids making bread rolls.'

'So, massaging me is like kneading?'

Yes, she thinks, *it's something I 'need'*. She knows she gives him massages willingly, too willingly. Can you ever have enough touch, reassurance?

'Not exactly, I remember you telling me that the French method is more a layering of the dough.'

'What an excellent memory.'

'Do you remember making fresh rolls the evening I fund-raised in the café bar? You were upset as your first girlfriend had died of a brain tumour and you said you had to get back to basics.'

'How the fuck do you remember so vividly?'

'You showed me a photo on your laptop screen of her with her daughter. Your ex-girlfriend had a beautiful open face. They were standing in a garden or park.'

'Yes, I treated her really badly towards the end. I don't want to hurt you. You know that don't you?'

'Yes,' and she bends over his head and skims a kiss. 'Let's just be quiet and let my fingers do the talking. Relax.'

Ella opens her hands wide in curvaceous strokes over his back then runs her fingers up and down his spine, circling in between the vertebrae, as he rests against the table.

'Are you sure you're okay?'

'Yes, I'm fine. Just enjoy it.'

Ella is enjoying the touch as much as she loves pressing the keys to make words flow onto the page, rather than the words stuttering, stuck in her gullet, choked with pain. This is pleasurable. As the massage ends, she lets her fingers flit over his back in a feathery action and then wraps him in a warm fluffy blanket so he doesn't get cold. He holds her hands as she leans over his shoulders and it feels blissful. She wants to stay there forever, gently held safe, her inner child protected.

He lets go. She moves away. Her discipline fixes a grin, allows practicality to set in.

'You clean your teeth first tonight so you don't catch a chill and then I'll do mine.'

'Thank you, it was great.'

When she goes to bed Ella recollects much earlier in their relationship that she had started reading *The World According to Garp* by John Irving, which he'd recommended, although he prefers *Hotel New Hampshire*, yes, she thinks that's the title.

She goes back to the day when he didn't answer his phone and the café bar was closed when it should have been open. She'd been brusque with his wife who had enquired how she was. She tells herself to be strong and not flirt with Patrick's emotions, which unknowingly she might have done, and arrives an hour later when the café bar is open.

She had gone in and he immediately made her tea.

'Let it brew for four minutes.'

He was smiling and added, 'Are you alright?'

'Yes, sort of.' She didn't add, *You gave me a fright this morning when you weren't open I thought you might have done something stupid.*

'You're not. What's up?'

'Nothing. It's fine now.'

'Are you sure?'

'Is your head okay?' He had a fresh cut on his forehead where he might have walked into something in a drunken stupor.

'Sore head but I'll be fine.'

'I've started reading John Irving's book, *The World According to Garp*.'

'Yes, I should reacquaint myself with that story.' Another customer came in. 'Sorry I'll have to go.'

'You've got a business to run.'

A week later she finished the book. It unearthed a gamut of emotions, lust for one. When she went to bed, it made it difficult for her to sleep. The bed was ravaged by the 'ultimate zipless fuck'. Her body squirmed, wanted, needed, demanded pulsating pleasure, which gave way to grief by early morning as she finished the book which was about fear, losing our children.

The tide ebbs away from Ella as she realises his estranged wife is coming to the café bar more frequently. His umbilical cord is still tied to her and the soft tissue of marriage is repairing; so, the healing sessions and their times alone together stop.

Patrick doesn't want to lose his children. His son has worked in the café bar but is now off travelling, trying to find out what he really wants to do. The other one is living in the Big Smoke.

Is that the reason he never really breaks away from his estranged wife? They even had a period of reciprocity when she helped in the café whilst Anneke had a week's holiday.

Ella writes about it.

You greet me

she greets me

asks if I'm okay

reply in the affirmative

we smile

you and her together

is as it should be.

I eat my salad

talk to the staff

say goodbye as you

sit on the bench, cigarettes in hand,

wish you both a nice day.

Your wedding ring

glints in the heat

I turn and walk the other way

rucksack slung on my back

the road is clear ahead

our diversion negotiated

when ice skimmed.

Now my skin is sun blessed

a yellow circle in a blue sky

my dress swirls white blue green

hers blue and white striped.

Now he is here, under Ella's roof, but for how long? Her hands relish being able to touch, savour his skin. She knows she doesn't want to cause any harm, just look after him and, in return, be hugged.

He would be listening to TED talks now in his room opposite hers. Her mind wanders to the word he used – Pantheism. Yes, she had looked it up, 'Pantheism: that God and universe are identical; the heathen worship of all gods.' Patrick used this word and she didn't query what it meant. He's more academic than she. In Paris the Panthéon is a building dedicated to the illustrious dead.

Ella's belief is in a super-human being, something beyond us, spiritual; wanting to spread happiness, being kind and considerate, dutiful when love is difficult. She's been a dutiful daughter looking after her dying dad. Patrick believes love is giving and expecting nothing in return. She knows that she has often given, happily, but now she is beginning to accept that she deserves to be cherished, protected. She wants the hugs that embrace her wellbeing. She cherishes every day he stays at hers.

Patrick adjusts the thermostat. 'It's probably healthy, but my house is warmer.'

Patrick has lost a lot of weight. He's tall and skinny. She can't believe he's once been twenty stone. He doesn't really eat. Preparing food all day, sometimes he thinks he's eaten when he's probably just had a nibble here and there. He doesn't expect her to cook for him and rarely eats with her. So, Ella thinks back fondly to the times he does share food with her.

There was the disaster with overcooked fish. He'd eaten it, jokingly asking, 'Is this cauliflower cheese?'

She'd blushed and gently smacked him on the arm. The other meals she'd made were all fine. He eats fast and likes more salt than her. After all, why should she be frightened just because he's a cook?

'I'm sorry but I should have defrosted the fish, it's gone all stringy.'

'String they might well use to fix bait on.'

She stays quiet. She wasn't going to play with his pun on words.

She thinks how she had provided good, plain, nourishing food for her family and for Tony during their time together, every day apart from the very occasional meal out. He'd always preferred her cooking and was more comfortable in his home environment.

Robert had liked her cooking too and when they divorced she remembers him asking, 'Could you show Susan how to cook pressed tongue please?'

'I suggest she looks in an old-fashioned recipe book,' was her reply. She'd learned from watching her grandmother.

Ella is back with Patrick. The room is warmer and he's toying with the sweet potato.

'I'm sorry; I've gone off sweet potato.'

'No worries.' She scrapes it off his plate onto to hers.

'I'll eat it, can't bear waste.'

'What's up?'

'It's just I feel I can't do anymore with the campaign.'

The Community Centre, which was a vital resource for information, supporting life-long learning in her area, was under threat of closure. It was a place where she had done much of her writing. It gave structure to her life. A place she visited on four plus days a week.

'If there were more staff employed, investigative journalists might have helped. Reverse psychology is needed,' Patrick comments.

'I suppose it hit me more today because someone with mental health problems I met on the bus said, 'You will save the place, won't you?''

'You're not wonder woman; it's not your responsibility.'

Ella accepted that logically she couldn't save the Centre singlehanded, but emotionally she wanted to rescue that sense of community that it engendered. It was the same sense of community that Patrick was trying to establish in his café. Give customers an opportunity to meet new people face to face, rather than people interacting with their phones.

But she realises that Patrick is feeling down and she should turn her attention away from herself to him.

'I can feel you didn't have a good day either there's a sense of...'

'I just feel a bit flat that's all.'

'Let me give you a massage.'

'Look you're tired. You've had a busy day.'

Patrick takes the dishes out washes them and brings her a glass of water.

'Massaging you relaxes me,' which is the truth; it did. She loves it.

'Okay, if you insist.'

Patrick takes his shirt off. Ella starts with a gentle touch.

'Just get in there and crack the pain out.'

She does as she is told, but her digits, although strong, ache with the effort and instinctively she knows that although he likes her fingers going in hard it won't be as intimate a feeling for her.

'Is the pressure okay, or am I hurting?'

'No, it's fine. You could do it harder, but don't hurt yourself.'

It's as though Patrick accepts that pain and pleasure go together.

Ella knows that cracking bones can mean things are going back in place but she's no osteopath or a sport's masseuse. It goes against her nature. It reminds her too much of herself being used to relieve sexual frustration; being trussed up like a chicken and being fucked by Robert, being penetrated, bored through, objectified; or Tony cajoling her to oblige him with 'just a quickie' when he needed to relax. It was bending the letters out of alignment, out of shape, contorting what she felt Patrick needed.

It is as though Patrick wants the brutality which will realign him and, like foamed water sloughing the ground, like a discarded snake's skin, remove the pain. Ella eases off the pressure as she gets to Patrick's head.

'I suggest you put your shirt back on so you don't feel cold.'

He dutifully does. She rubs his temples. He takes her fingers and places them further down and circles her fingers.

'There, that's right.'

She repeats the massage of his temples several times to get the position fixed in her mind. It becomes a reflex action. She finishes the massage and says, 'It's time for bed. We both need our sleep.'

Patrick nods, 'I'm whacked, but relaxed thanks to you.'

She smiles, 'Sleep well.'

'And you too.'

****

The vessel is getting leather-hard but is still very fragile. By adding a little moisture she can make any final adjustments before it dries out completely. If she uses any force it will shatter. She cradles it in her hand, feels for any lumpiness on the surface, which she delicately peels away. Now she can let the surface dry out and heal.

Sometimes she sees a plant she thinks has died. Her initial reaction is to get rid of it. She has learned to wait and reassess the situation. On inspecting the plant more closely there will be a tiny bud or leaf, the possibility of nurturing it back to health. She knows how there are day to day changes in her garden and it gives her pleasure to see a closed bud, hidden and shy, gradually unfolding, bursting from its sheath and giving itself up to the elements.

****

Chapter Nine

Next morning Patrick appears with his washing. Ella gets on with her own laundry and shopping then pops into the café before drama class, part of her weekly routine.

'You didn't stay away long.'

Ella hands over some sweet stuff for the café. Patrick offers to pay and she accepts.

'Anneke is unwell so she won't be in.'

'You'll manage on your own. Believe in yourself. I believe in you.'

Later that evening Patrick sends a text asking, hypothetically, if he could stay the night.

'Of course.'

Ella prepares a meal, marinates the prawns in garlic, ginger and soya sauce and prepares the vegetables, cooks the rice, de-pips the pomegranate, what a kerfuffle, not with a pin one seed at a time like Patrick said he'd witnessed as a child. Now Jamie Oliver beats the cut up pomegranate with a wooden spoon and the ruby seeds are released. Ella adds persimmon, grapes and a strawberry to each dish.

Patrick's longer than expected but Ella makes a dream board, sits listening to Radio Four and relaxes – something she rarely does. Later she texts him and asks when he might be coming back? He explains he's 'Tidying, won't be too long.'

'No worries.'

Patrick comes back not expecting a meal but joins her and eats enthusiastically saying it's tasty, although adding a bit more soya sauce.

'I'm happy my son is coming down from London and I'll see him in the café. I also talked to my mum for over an hour and persuaded her to go to a party in the big house, which she will enjoy. She admits to being a snob, regrets not visiting a friend because her husband was working class.'

Patrick clears the table and washes up. Ella asks for a cuddle.

His arms are wide open and the vibration is so different from yesterday. She allows her tears of joy to fall behind her closed bedroom door. His ashen face of yesterday is full of hope. He's had a good day in the café, no longer feeling flat.

They are both in their separate bedrooms as she thinks of the weeks when Patrick made a special smoothie for Stevie, a friend of hers dying of cancer. Towards the end he preferred orange juice. She recalls popping into the café.

'What's the matter?'

'Stevie died in the early hours of this morning. One of his daughters has just texted me.'

Patrick hugs her and gently strokes Ella's tear-stained face.

'It was peaceful. Last night I popped into the hospital to see him. He had some juice and then he was sleepy. I stroked his face till he went to sleep and left.'

'You did everything you could.'

'I have to go now. I have got to run the games club.'

She's glad that she has those moments of structure in life that at times keep her diverted, like rungs in a ladder they allow her to hold onto the everyday, although she also likes spontaneous days when things just happen.

Ella recalls receiving a text later that same day: 'How u doing?'

And when he came 'home,' he immediately cuddled and held her, let her burrow deep down into his jacket. She was safe.

'He really enjoyed your drinks,' she muttered between the tears. She didn't add, *He knew about you and was pleased I had someone who makes me happy.*

'He's at rest.'

'My daughter's gone over to see the children; she's a good girl.'

And you are kind and compassionate.'

Ella managed a smile.

'He liked *Morse, Dixon of Dock Green*, which I used to watch with my Gran.'

Patrick strokes her hair and hugs her again.

'I have to stand on tiptoes because you are so tall compared to me.'

They'd both smiled. She went to sleep.

Ella is turned on at the thought of having a lover. She feels safe and respected by Patrick. Well, you only have one life, so why not? It doesn't really matter does it? Just thrust any doubts aside and do it. What could happen? She won't die. So when she is doing her shopping in town next day she gets some KY Jelly. She has no secrets, not many anyway, from her daughter who says, 'You can't use that it will go all sticky. It's used for enemas.'

They laugh. Her daughter says, 'Sex is funny, it's never perfect. You'll have to go to the sex shop and get some Liquid Silk.' She looks up the place on her mobile phone, and the price, and says, 'Try a small bottle and then you can graduate to the larger one if necessary. Don't want any wastage.'

The shop is closed that day, but the next day Ella ventures in and is confounded by leather gear, bullet-shaped juice, kinky stuff; she's embarrassed, but then notices another shelf right next to the counter, with lubricants. The man in the shop is short, has pierced ears, short back and sides revealing a tinge of grey in his mousey hair. He's dressed in dun brown and takes little notice of her browsing. Ella peruses the shelf and sees the Liquid Silk. There's an offer on the larger one but she takes the small one. Meanwhile a male customer has his items put in a discreet brown paper bag. She hands over her small bottle, passes over the money, not quibbling that it's more than it said on the app. He asks if she would like a bag.

'No thank you it will slip into my rucksack without a problem.'

Ella exits from the shop, rucksack on her back. She wonders how many mature women visit the shop. At least the shopkeeper's expression remained unperturbed, no, she means undisturbed.

The day is like any other. She goes into the café, has some homemade soup (chick pea and brown lentils) with seeded sourdough bread, and a health-giving smoothie with celery, apple, lime, spirulina, pea protein, to set her up for the day. She's walked Holly, prepared her daughter's meal, waited for her granddaughter and taken her to extra maths.

That night Patrick phones, 'Sorry, I won't be able to come back home. Need to sort something out with my estranged wife.'

She's always said he would be in the shit if he didn't tell the truth, so she accepts it, trying to seem unaffected by the news, but a tinge of disappointment sweeps through her. Well, more than a tinge. She thinks that on this night they could have made love but she knows she shouldn't make a fuss.

'That's fine, no worries.' Yet she thinks he could have told her in the morning rather than now and she could have gone out, done something else, not felt cheated – not cheated exactly, it was only in her mind after all, not in reality. She'd envisaged them making love and it seemed so real, a real possibility, even when she remembers those times he's gently chided her. She always took his rejection – was it rejection or protection? – with a smile, a faint shrug of the shoulders. He always apologised for his school boyish remark that the Rabbit was the most popular tool. Ella has never fancied something mechanical. She remembers from the distant past going to a Tupperware party which actually was a cover for selling Anne Summers' products; the Gold 007 being the most sought-after model. Its vibration was of that of a jet aeroplane and one might well take off but, her lips pursed and her shoulders shrugged... no, not for her.

That evening she busies herself with sorting out papers, takes the bottle of Liquid Silk from the rucksack and goes to bed. Maybe she could give it a try. Sometimes it was difficult to get to sleep.

And this was as good a way as any. She opens the bottle and, indeed, it's very smooth; she lubricates her clitoris. She pictures his penis erect between her breasts, her stimulating the tip, caressing its swelling tender flesh, teasing it in and out of her mouth. Sucking his cock and feeling its contours, feeling the urgency of his thrusts. He's about to come when he puts it in her cunt. She touches the pre-cum slithered between her breasts. Her nipples are erect. Ella imagines focusing on his eyes. They're both panting, gasping, wanting each other. She experiences that exquisite anticipation, knowing it's gone too far, the feeling of ululation, the orgasm is starting. Revelling in that liquidity, groaning, wanting to hold onto that bliss as their bodies shudder with relief, she releases screams of, 'Yes, yes!'

She smiles as she remembers Patrick saying, 'Make sure the erotic bits are good that's what will sell the book.'

Now she can sleep. In her heart she knows this may only be for her but, nonetheless, it's beautiful and makes her feel good.

****

The bowl is now leather-hard. Her fingers repetitively stroke the outer surface, gently burnishing the clay. The clay reacts to the rhythmic movements by darkening in colour – starts to glisten. The caressed molecules of clay have let go, like her being hugged in Patrick's arms, fear is released and their hidden notes now surface.

****

CHAPTER TEN

When Ella initially met Patrick, it was his first venture at running a café bar. Ella longed to be alone with him other than in the regular healing sessions she gave him (in his cubbyhole above the bar). She did occasionally go into the café bar at night and one night, when he was alone, he put his favourite piece of work on the big screen. It meant they were together but there was still a barrier. Sometimes they watched cookery programmes together on his computer. But on this occasion he'd had the big screen up.

'Pedro Meyer has one of my favourite bodies of work, one that I showed to my students, some of whom photographed their own parents' old age and death, and became renowned as a result.'

It's the story of Pedro's parents, Liesel and Ernesto, from their engagement and marriage to their deaths. On the screen is a torn picture, where the wife is missing, torn off by the Nazis. The other photograph, intact, shows them sitting on reclining chairs in the garden.

Ernesto is now slumped on the toilet and Liesel trying to soothe the searing pain. It reminds Ella of Patrick's father trying to change himself and getting shit everywhere with the carer near breaking point.

Liesel and Ernesto's faces are full of apprehension before the doctor's diagnosis of cancer and finding out that Ernesto's disease has spread too far for any treatment. He has only weeks to live. His resolution was to be strong, and death waited for three years to reap his spirit.

This reminds Ella of her mother being told she had terminal cancer. Her mother persuaded the consultant to shield Ella from the fact. In the end her mother proved the doctor wrong, living far longer than he predicted.

She also recalls Patrick being scared that he could have prostate cancer, or problems with his liver but refusing to go to the doctor. She's given up trying to persuade him. It is his life, his responsibility.

Ernesto was a toy salesman who moved to Mexico, then travelled to Japan and sold items from porcelain, even a motorbike. In the early days he arranged a selection of dolls in his hotel bedroom. The display reminds Ella of her arranging Larry the Lamb and a Chad Valley doll called Gloria on a bench under her granny's apple tree.

The love and gentleness between Liesel and Ernesto is so palpable; the mouths that nearly kiss. Ella sees a picture of intimacy, yet the camera also gives a feeling of distance. A charming picture captures them dancing together. Each and every day, they go for little strolls outside. His pockets are full of candy for children. There's a poignant picture of Ernesto being helped to walk, painfully putting one foot in front of another, juxtaposed with a baby learning to take her first steps. Joy and pathos hand in hand.

Ella longs for this gentleness in a loving relationship, and she watches Patrick's eyes light up whenever he sees a child or toddler. Is he trying to embrace *his* inner child or his children, who he adores? His face never fails to beam, even when depressed, when children are around.

Liesel is shocked, weakened by the terminal diagnosis, and so Ernesto becomes strong. He comes back to his apartment and his son asks how he would like his portrait taken. His dad says, 'flying', so his shirt sleeves are raised and flapping in the air. Gradually the roles reverse and Liesel becomes the nurturer. Hands are always touching. The cameraman, the son, holds the camera in one hand, his dad's in the other. Sometimes Ernesto grabs his son's hand so hard it becomes blue under the grip. His dad is holding onto life. Ella touches Patrick's hand, but there is no response, even to stroking, so she lets it go.

How ironic, the son has just taken a picture of a new-born baby and is then called to another hospital in the same town, where his mother has been diagnosed with a brain tumour and haemorrhage. He has to make a life or death decision: either to opt for an immediate operation or allow her to die. He opts for the operation, and they shave her head, a reminder of concentration camps, but ten days later she is wearing a lacy mop cap. She looks elegant. Her hair re-grows. She relearns to do her makeup, a tedious and repetitive task as her coordination is compromised. Still she perseveres.

Ella remembers her mother's hair growing back after chemotherapy; it was much darker. That year she was in total remission.

Ernesto's eye closes as the tumour spreads and he covers up the good eye to open the bad, like Ella closed off her physical needs for affection and channelled them into giving. Liesel's tumour grows back and now she's paralysed on the left side and has to be spoon fed. She dies. Her husband is not told about it but innately knows. He refuses food, has difficulty breathing. Nine weeks later he dies.

The lasting feeling is of such tenderness. In the picture where the grandson is with his grandfather, pointing a finger playfully at his granddad's nose, Ernesto was having a good day. His delight shows at being able to visit his son's flat, with his wife, for just an hour.

Ella took her children regularly to visit her mum when she was terminally ill and the film has captured the same joy her children gave her mother.

Patrick says at the end of the film, 'Let's face it, we all have to die.'

'We all have to learn to survive, live.'

Well, she had to learn to live. Yes, she'd grieved, but she knew life was precious. Tony wanted her to be free of unnecessary worry, and now Ella tries to make the most of her life.

Patrick looks at Ella, 'I'm sorry I've upset you.'

'It's okay. I saw my mum die and dad too. The love is palpable. Those fleeting expressions lit the screen. I could feel the tenderness between them.'

She puts her hand on his knee and then removes it.

I wish I could see my parents more, but it's difficult to leave the business,' he says.

'Maybe when Anneke is more familiar with the work involved, you'll be able to visit them.'

'Yes, perhaps, but that will take time.'

'Have you got pictures of your parents?'

'Not really.'

'My mother chose to wear a broderie anglaise nightie with daisies when she was dying. My dad wore a navy-blue blazer, checked shirt, yellow tie, grey trousers, yellow socks, in his coffin. He took what we thought was his last breath and my daughter and I kissed him goodbye and then, as in life, he took another, always had to have the last word. It made me and my daughter laugh.'

She also admits, 'Ernesto looked a bit like my uncle who was a prisoner of war, forced to build the Burma railway. He came back to England weighing five stone.' And she added, 'He died at the same age as my dad, ninety-four.'

Patrick said, 'Your uncle learned to survive, live.'

Ella nods her head and remembers Richard. 'You know the first person I had a crush on when I was sixteen, died.'

'How did he die?'

'In a car crash. He would have been a vegetable if he'd survived. His parents turned his life support off. They found my love letters from boarding school. I remember my mother telling me, when I went out to Wad Medani south of Khartoum.'

'What were your parents doing there?'

'My dad worked for the British Council. He was in the Sudan Defence Force during the war. I flew over in a Viscount, a pre-jet plane.' She added that detail because she knows Patrick likes old planes.

'Interesting. What did your first boyfriend do?'

'He was a teacher, twice my age and part time archaeologist. We went visiting shallow graves. They buried people with what they thought they would need in the next life, cooking pots and so on. I found a sloughed-off snake skin and ran out of the grave. I was hysterical. Richard caught me and hugged me until I stopped trembling.'

'So, are you scared of snakes now?'

'Not too keen. As a teenager I had repeated nightmares of being hung over a hissing snake pit.'

'Freud would have had something to say about that.'

'I touched a python in Khartoum zoo and it was warm and not slimy.'

'Did that make you feel better?'

'No, not really.'

She thought of the incident as a teenager when she'd gone into the nave of the church and one of her dad's acquaintances revealed his flaccid penis in between the covers of a prayer book, her feeling of absolute horror and disgust. She'd walked away in disbelief, never told anyone.

'Ella, you're full of fascinating stories.'

'I've been lucky in that I travelled a lot with my parents.'

She looks at her watch, aware she shouldn't overstay her welcome because they both had to be up early in the morning.

'It's getting late. I should go home.'

Patrick hugs her goodbye. She is reluctant to let go but, as she feels his grip loosen, she moves away.

Ella recalls how Tony gave her that sense of security when holding her hand, but Patrick was the first man who had embraced her wellbeing with a hug.

Ella returns into the now. She is early for writing group. There is insufficient time to go home. She goes to the café and knocks. Patrick is sitting at his computer with the window blinds drawn. He looks up, smiles, and comes to open the door.

'Is it alright if I come in, I don't want to disturb you?'

'Of course, sit down, make yourself comfortable. I was just catching up on emails and stuff.'

She thinks, looking at the screen, that it might well have been motor racing he'd been watching.

'I won't disturb you. I'll get on with some writing.'

Ella empties her rucksack and gets out her notepad and biro, unlike Patrick who prefers a pen. She'd given him a pen for his birthday, towards the end of February.

'I've started the reporter's book you gave me for Christmas.' Ella shows him the black round-cornered moleskin reporter's book. I made jottings when I was in Liverpool.'

'Good.'

She thinks back to when Patrick gave the book to her, a Christmas present, a thank you for what she had done for him. The quote on the inside cover read, 'A book for modern people on the go, whose identity is linked with nomadic objects.' He'd always said Ella's home reflected doing stuff whereas his marital home was a museum of artefacts. Patrick is nomadic in that recently he's stayed mainly at Anneke's since he's started his new café, or sometimes with other friends or even on the café floor.

The reporter's book was originally produced by a small French bookbinder who supplied stationary shops in Paris. The notebooks were bought by literati and artists. They transformed their scribbling, drawings, into books, paintings. Ella mused on how Patrick loved all things French. He'd trained as a chef in France. When the Brexit vote came in he made a tricolour sandwich to express his solidarity with the Europeans, the French in particular.

She remembers that this notebook was reproduced by a Milanese publisher. Patrick had bought another notebook from Italy as a present for his dad. He'd shown it to Ella when he was at hers. It was brown and embossed with brownish red, well, burnt umber patterning. He'd said, 'You know I stole this notebook back from my dad. Well, he can't use it anymore and I meant to jot down his memoirs in it but, when it came to it, they were too pretentious. It never happened. They were unreadable. Now it's mine.'

He showed Ella the front page where on one corner he had written, 'I love you Dad.'

She gave Patrick a hand-knitted scarf for Christmas, entwined with love. Something practical; blue, grey, brown, reflecting the colours he liked. She thinks back to her knitted Christmas stocking on her bed, which leads her back into her childhood, when she broke her promise to her mother by opening her Christmas stocking. Since then she has tried never to break a promise.

Ella fingered her black reporter's book from Patrick. She'd put the label in the memento section 'Dear Ella, Happy Christmas 2017. Thank You. Love Patrick xxx.'

He'd not bought his parents Christmas presents but said, 'There are service stations on the way.'

Ella is aware of a clatter of utensils. She looks up and Patrick is starting to cook carrot cake. She says in passing, 'Saw Tom Woods at the Open Eye gallery.'

'Yes, I've heard of him.'

'He does pictures of ordinary people making a journey or queuing at a bus stop, waiting for the ferry, or on a bus with reflections, refractions of faces.'

'My mad friend who used to be a famous photographer has started a body of work, concentrating on just one person that he meets that day, getting to know them, and taking lots of photographs of them.'

'What a lovely idea.'

'Yes, he makes them feel special.'

Ella is thinking, *like you make me feel*. She gets on with her writing and sees him collecting ingredients, weighing them and his arm whirling them round in the bowl. They work in comfortable silence. She is unaware of time, till there is an agitated knock on the door. It's Anneke. Patrick lets her in. Ella says a cursory, 'Hello.'

'Hello.'

Ella feels a that a barrier has been lifted, the outer case of seed has split and now they might reconnect or, like clay that was cracked, can be invisibly mended with a mixture of sugar and clay. It feels good, sweet. Ella persevering with saying hello and goodbye to Anneke, although ignored until now, has been worth it.

Ella asks, 'How are you?'

'Very well thank you, Ella.'

Anneke joins Patrick in the back kitchen and Patrick asks, 'How did you get on?'

Ella continues to write. They both love the same man in different ways but he would never be totally theirs. Patrick works well with Anneke. They understand their little foibles and she is as necessary to his wellbeing as Ella. It has been difficult to keep being polite, and being ignored, but worthwhile. Everyone deserves to be happy. Ella's and Anneke's relationship was back to being amicable. Ella was glad.

She concentrates on her writing and after ten minutes she gets up and says, 'Goodbye Anneke and Patrick.' Ella closes the door of the café behind her. It's pouring.

****

Now the burnished bowl is ready to be fired. Tempered in the heat of the kiln, it's becoming stronger. The temperature is safely pre-set on the kiln, the rise in heat is gradual. The bowl emerges intact after the kiln has cooled down and the polished bits are highlighted by the biscuit firing.

Reading a recipe Patrick takes the ingredients in his hands and weighs them one by one. Feels their texture, smells the aroma, imagines how flavours, colours combine. The excitement of the palate lies in the moment of creation giving that extra piquancy.

Death, dying is threaded throughout her work and Pedro Meyer's film is the link that twists and intertwines endings, transformations, like the ivy in Ella's garden. Sometimes it looks beautiful, other times it sinews its way into her brain disturbing her equilibrium, stirring feelings of guilt. Yet death and life, like shadows, or highlights in paintings and photos, are qualities which delineate the whole, like the black grout filling the interstices in the mosaics redefines striated colours.

****

Chapter Eleven

Ella is aware that her writing groups and games group at the Centre allow a mix of people to feel safe, express their feelings, and socialise with others. She is a facilitator, enabler, although she hates those words. She's just happy helping people.

There is an atmosphere of camaraderie between everyone. Ella is always willing to put herself on the line by reading her work, even if it is sometimes banal. Steven and David, who play games, have special needs. They enjoy playing Scrabble together and occasionally Categories. On the adjoining table they're playing Upwords and there is the casual exchange of banter between the tables. 'How are you doing?' 'What kind of week have you had?' Hints are given from the other table where Ella's group is playing Categories. The objective is to find towns, animals, titles of films, beginning with a certain letter. David is good at Scrabble and Steven is better at Categories.

The writing styles in her group are very diverse. Most are happy to share their work. Over time their confidence grows, like plants flourishing in her garden. Even those that initially feel intimidated by the thought of writing words on paper find that their sieved or dredged words are applauded. Some use rhythm, rhyme, others are inspired by debate, an unconscious stream, moved by photographs, words, objects which Ella provides as inspiration, or thoughts triggered by past memories. The final exercise of a group poem on a set topic, gives cohesion to the class. The work they choose to submit will be collated for publication in an anthology, to raise funds for the Centre, and also be heard at a public performance. Compiling the anthology has become an annual ritual in Ella's life, harvesting the group's diversity. Ella is very grateful for a fellow volunteer's help in editing and formatting the anthology.

Was it the doubt of the Centre's future which was making her question Patrick's motives? Was he trying to take advantage of her too? The Centre was happy for her to do things for free and get her to encourage people to use the community facility, although the core values such as the careers service were axed to save money. It's a holistic service and run on a one to one basis together with lots of courses ranging from art, exercise classes and IT. She has been warned by the staff not to put all her energy into the campaign to save the service, but to look after her needs. Ella can't help thinking of the analogy of the air safety message: put your mask on before helping someone else.

Ella realises that cuts locally, and elsewhere, are tied into political manoeuvres that are not in the public arena. Yet she finds it almost impossible not to be pro-active and put her energy into the community; hasn't her role in the Centre become integral to her own well being?

The longest serving Centre staff members, unsettled by the uncertainty of their future, have found other jobs. She doesn't blame them, but feels sad their expertise will be lost. She wishes them luck. The Centre's focus will inevitably change but it's still a place that encourages people to use the premises for social activities. Ella realises that doubt has made her seek even more control in her own life.

This Centre gave her a sense of purpose when widowhood first spliced her roots. Naturally she had family duties, which made her feel needed, but the Centre gave her a sense of autonomy. It was different. Ella doesn't want it slowly to wither away and die, lose its identity.

Patrick is living in Ella's home on a purely temporary basis. But somehow, she feels an unease stir inside her. She is questioning herself; is he using her like a sex object? Is he naturally charming or is it smarminess, wanting to please? Is it just for his personal benefit? Yet she had always said he was welcome to stay with her if he wanted.

'Patrick you know there's something I must clarify, so when one night we are both in, I would like to discuss a thing that's bothering me.'

Well, he is someone she trusts. She feels innately comfortable with him. However embarrassing it seems, she could talk to him about anything. Yet these thoughts are niggling inside her. Could it have stemmed from him complementing her when a friend had done a belly dance at a fundraising event?

'Your friend's technically good, but you're a natural, it oozes through you.'

She just lets her body react to the music. The movements writhe within her. Just as they did on her recent visit to Liverpool when the guitarist played, 'Let it Be' for her. Does he find her sexy or does he just want to be with someone who accepts him, cares for him and where he feels safe; touches him but doesn't want to own him, won't abandon him. Does he seek unconditional love? Maybe that's what they've got in common?

So, a few days later he's sitting opposite her at the table in her home.

'So, you wanted to talk. I'm here, out with it, what's bothering you?'

She feels herself slam shut as though she's a writer who has been asked to write and in that instant her thoughts shudder, stutter. Maybe she shouldn't say anything. Her mouth tightens she bites her lip.

'I don't know where to begin. I don't even know I want to say anything.'

'Just spit it out.'

She feels the fear of criticism, of being belittled, rise in her throat. His eyes stare into hers. She meets his gaze, takes a deep breath. Is he taking advantage of her? She doesn't want to admit it. She has allowed the thought to play in her mind until it has become fixed, and she either needs to cut it out or ask him to leave. It's no more difficult than going into the sea, normally she edges her way in slowly, but sometimes she briskly plunges. So be it. Her gut has niggled at her brain, worming this doubt – now she has to confront it.

'I just have a feeling you maybe treating me like a sex object.'

Is she treating *him* like one, wanting him to fulfil her sexual desires? But that isn't true. She couldn't fancy anyone, she couldn't bloody talk to. She finds him attractive, yes, but it goes deeper than that. His body stiffens, his voice becomes defensive.

'Well, if that's the case we should stop the massages from now.'

She knows he likes the massages, they relax him.

'No, I don't want to. I enjoy giving massages. I don't know why the idea came into my head, but you know I have to say what I'm thinking. I'm sorry.' Why is she apologising yet again? She realises she loves having him there even though it's not that often.

'Why be sorry?' Patrick asks.

'I just don't want to feel used and I know now you are not using me.' *Any more than I am using you*, she thinks, *in that I love you being here, and the massages make me feel really close to you. Maybe more intimate than going to bed with you, although I'm tempted with the thought.* She ends up saying, 'Maybe it's my prudish upbringing coming out?'

'You're anything but prudish. Do you remember the first time you admitted you fancied me?'

Ella smiles, 'Yes, I'd been in the pub with my friend and told her about how I was feeling about you and showed her some of my writing. She was shocked. I'd had a couple of drinks and was quite happy. She asked me, "Are you sure you want to do this? What if he rejects you?"'

Ella has this intuitive feeling, you could call it sixth sense, that she should just tell him. 'She let me come over to yours, asking me to call her or at least text, whatever the time, and let her know how it went and that I got home safely.'

Patrick recalls the occasion and says, 'You arrived. I was quite surprised because you were a little tipsy.'

'You poured me another beer. I handed you the sheet of paper.'

'I said I would read it later upstairs.'

' "No, now! I want to see your expression." I was quite adamant. And by then my hands were shaking uncontrollably, but it was too late to take my writing back. You'd begun to read.'

'I said I was flattered, and embarrassed, that you wanted to fuck me.'

'No, I've never really wanted to fuck you. I admit I fancied you, but I didn't want to fuck you.'

'Really? It's okay if you'd wanted to.'

'No, deep down I don't think I've ever really wanted to. We've both been self-disciplined in our ways. I knew you made me feel different about myself, sexually alive, but something was stopping me going the whole way. Yes, I would masturbate, fantasise about you. It was never with anyone else.'

'I'm glad about that.' His eyes glance at his watch, 'My God is that the time? Look I'm sorry I've got to put in the order for the café. I won't be long.' He goes upstairs to his room.

Ella's mind wanders and she thinks of Patrick's inability to focus, always being distracted. He's told her his school reports said he could do well but lacked concentration. He had queried if it was ADHD.

If she hadn't removed his stuff from the room because of his vituperative text, would he have ever made the time to do so? Was his procrastination, a way of saying he didn't really want to leave either?

Her gut tells her he was never going to become her lover and not to make another mistake. It wasn't what she really wants. Ella begins talking to herself as though Patrick was still there.

'I suppose I'm old fashioned and couldn't just fuck you and get you out of my system. I nearly got to the point. Then I think you texted and told me you needed to visit your wife. Maybe I respect myself and you too much. I know I push and pull, but deep down I don't want to ruin a friendship, or my inspiration to write. That way I can find myself, and maybe a bit of you, between the covers of a book.'

Patrick comes down, 'Can I have a shower please?'

'Of course, you don't have to ask.'

'I stink.'

'I like your smell. I'll give you a massage afterwards.'

'That would be lovely.'

Ella puts up the massage couch, puts the towels on top for him to lie on and covers them with the soft blanket from his bed and the patchwork knitted blanket on top. She turns off the main lights and has a jasmine-scented candle burning on the table and a small bedside light beside the massage couch with her oils. She turns the thermostat up and puts the heating on constant.

Patrick emerges from the shower room with a towel neatly tied round his waist, smelling of cedar wood and salty spray.

He slips between the covers on the massage table.

'Are you sure you are warm enough?'

'Yes, I'm fine thanks.'

Patrick closes his eyes, sighs out and relaxes. Intuitively her fingers massage his brow and concentrate on his temples. She recognises she has hit the spot as a gentle moan emanates, and she circles them tenderly. The pressure is soft but firm. She wants him to sleep, relax.

She massages the outlines of his face, and gently goes over his eyes, while the eyebrows are fingered with more pressure. Using thumb and index finger, she stimulates his earlobes. Although he's relaxed, she feels a momentary tingle, hears soft sighs, and sees the slightest curve of his mouth. Her fingers gently make upward movements, from the chin over the face, caressing his unshaven skin.

She uncovers his clavicles, runs her hand along his breastbone and moves his head to the right, allowing her hand to stroke the breast, go under his back and swirl along his neck in one elongated stroke. She holds his neck and head in her hands. This is done on both sides. When the head is in the central position then she can embrace his neck with both hands, stretch it gently, pulling the head towards her breasts and letting it rest in her hands, taking its weight. She uses her core muscles. She can sense by the change in his breathing that this pleasures them both.

She massages each arm from wrist to elbow with fluid strokes and then, cosseting the elbow with the outer part of her palm, she massages the hollow. The upper arm is treated as the forearm. The whole arm is stretched and moved from the shoulder. Then the hand is massaged, each digit held and stroked, and the palm as well. She loves doing this as rarely, if ever, do they hold hands, but his hand is curled and relaxed when she massages, not pulling away from her. She goes down the bones in the hand leading to the fingers, stimulating the immune system; she pulls each digit through her hand, which is clasped round like a fist, gently pummelling the tip, and then giving each finger a final pull. The palm is rubbed with her thumb going into the fleshy parts, followed by the whole back of the hand.

Ella strokes his whole arm, sandwiching his hand between hers, repeating this action several times as though enclosing the arm in a total caress; she will do the feet and legs later. But before this she uncovers his chest and belly. Quick, fluent, alternate strokes, opened-palmed, flow from each side of his chest. She circles his stomach, which is soft and flat, with her hands, one following the other and crossing over each other in a rhythmic motion, ending the sequence with placing her hands over his belly button. She covers him up. The massage is like a choreographed dance and she can improvise where she chooses to linger.

She massages each leg individually with upward strokes, one hand following the other, and then the thumb splaying to the side aiding the circulation. Like massaging the hands, she caresses each leg in flowing strokes and sandwiches his feet between her hands. Each foot is massaged, the toes circled and the pads underneath pummelled. The arch is stroked, stimulating the kidneys, the ankle bones circled. At the end she places her open palms, allowing the warmth of her hands to seep into the soles of his feet. She is grounding his energy, allowing them both to luxuriate in these moments of stillness.

She asks him to turn over onto his front while she goes and washes her hands. She uncovers his back. Now her elongated strokes over his back entwine them together as she pulls his body towards her. Ella leans over the massage couch as she caresses his back as if they were lying together. She runs her hands up and down his spine rhythmically. She loves this pas de deux and repeats it leaning her body fully over the couch, savouring holding and slipping his body through her hands. She can feel her whole body tingling with the joy of being at one with him, yet she is fully clothed and he, like clay in her hands, is being shaped, fingered and touched. He will hold onto life, be alive; something she couldn't do for Tony.

She remembers the first time he had a massage. She'd smiled when he apologised, 'I'm sorry I'm so hairy.'

'I don't mind,' and she didn't. The hairs were soft and fine and didn't stop the fluidity of the massage.

Her hands swirl Patrick's back in flowing figures of eight, then her thumbs circle following the length of his spine, moving from the bottom to the top, her whole hand holding his body as she sweeps her hands to begin the movement again, repeating it many times. Her hands fan up and down his spine, her digits caress the sides of his body in a swaying movement; as she stands at the side, her arms rub his back up and down in alternate strokes that increase the blood flow. The strokes are vigorous; she follows by pressing her wrist to elbow of her arms from the centre to the neck and lower spine, stretching him, holding energy between the points for several moments. She feels him sigh out, completely letting go. It's followed by a moment of stillness and healing, before she feathers his back with her finger tips. This movement indicates this part of the massage is coming to an end. A letting go.

She covers him with the blanket and massages his legs. Her hands move up each leg and down to his feet and toes, digging her thumb into the meridians, the middle section of each ankle up the shin of the leg to the knee, and stroking outwards with her thumb. This stroke is followed by the palms of each hand swiftly and firmly sliding, one followed by the other from his ankle to knee. His upper leg is equally stimulated as the lower half and then each leg is stroked as a whole, encapsulating his foot in her hands.

The legs are covered and his foot is massaged, each toe circled in both directions, the arch stroked upwards, the sides circled and finally his foot sandwiched between her hands. Then she covers Patrick totally in the blanket. His eyes are closed; occasionally he snores, dropping off to sleep. She sits on a chair and puts her hands on his outstretched feet, allowing the warmth from them to heal, to ground him. He is totally relaxed and she doesn't want to move.

But after several minutes she goes over his body with her hands above him and where her fingers vibrate, she leaves them there until the tingling stops. With a gentle touch she moves down his body, wiping any negativity away, lingering for a few seconds on his feet, and then removes her hands totally. He keeps his eyes closed, his breathing is rhythmic and she just sits and smiles thinking she would like to have him lie in bed next to her – just being cuddled – if only.

He mutters as he reluctantly stretches his arms out of the blanket, then wraps them under again, 'That was absolutely lovely, are you sure you're okay?'

After several minutes he sits up and she clambers onto the massage table opposite him, making sure his body is wrapped up. She lays her head in his lap. Massaging him must have relaxed her, and she doesn't realise how tired she really is. She's happy. She's loves doing this, touching him. She finds her breathing deepening and several minutes later she feels him gently stroking her head. She must have gone to sleep.

That's a moment she'll never forget.

'It's time for bed,' Patrick says.

She smiles. It has been perfect. She doesn't want that feeling to end. Neither does she want to spoil that serene moment, so she obediently gets off the couch and says, 'Beddy-byes. I'll clean my teeth first while you stay warm under the covers and then you can use the bathroom.

As he wishes her goodnight he says, 'Don't worry I turned off the heating as you've forgotten. It's on the normal cycle again.'

In the past he's said, 'Massage can only lead in one direction.' He tended to use rhymes, once saying to Ella, 'My wife thinks I'm something rhyming with 'dock.'' She was really thick, not thinking of the obvious. He explains. She sniggers remembering her girlfriends saying, while they were out enjoying a meal, why didn't she give him a hand job while massaging him and make it impossible for him to say 'no.'

She doesn't know whether she'd be expert enough. It doesn't feel right. And tonight, well hadn't her fingers, her body oozed with want? But in a strange way it was too beautiful to spoil that feeling. It's an unconditionally loving act. No, 'act' was the wrong word, *gift*, yes, a gift that they both share because she gets as much joy giving as he does receiving. The hurt she feels dissipates, like sugar dissolves with heat, the granules no longer edgy but gliding into syrup. She knows how, when Patrick has a longing for sugar, he makes himself a cup of tea, puts in the sugar lumps, and stirs till they dissolve and savours the sweetness.

Realistically, she muses, would their love making be that great? He had a dodgy hip and hers was painful. Well, the pain moved from her hip to her knees in certain positions and if they were entwined it might mean both of them were in agony. Ella couldn't help chuckling to herself, although she had to admit that whilst he was staying there her aches and pains reduced considerably, sometimes disappearing altogether. It was probably the increased endorphins. He had left her home but she was glad she had kept her weight off. She'd lost a stone since being in love, which if nothing else was good for her arthritis.

She recalls they had initially got to know each other talking in the café bar that she visited with a friend each week after yoga. She had happened to mention to him that she practised healing and suggested maybe he would he like a trial session. He was sceptical, but she knew he was open to considering something alternative. She mentioned, 'I knew instinctively when my paternal grandfather had died. I rang the hospital a couple of minutes after it happened. I also knew a friend with motor-neurone disease was going to die. I had a funny experience of feeling very uneasy, not being able to concentrate for most of the day. Then suddenly, in the early hours of the morning, the feeling of unease dispersed and I knew.'

'What happened?'

'I rang her sister and said, 'Joyce has died, hasn't she?''

'Yes. peacefully in the night, or the early hours of the morning, the sheets were unruffled.'

Patrick had smiled enigmatically.

'Well let's see how we go, when would you like to give me healing?'

'Monday mornings, early, would suit me.'

Ella was so nervous at her first session; it stopped her natural intuition from coming to the fore. She asked him to take three deep breaths before she started, she did as well and then she asked him to breathe normally. For the first time ever, her breaths were slightly raspy, nervous.

'Are you okay?'

Ella reassures him, 'Yes I'm fine.' She doesn't want to admit she's anxious. She's afraid he won't enjoy the session, might not want another one. She gives him a visualisation of an oak trunk with him resting his back against it, the fragrance of bluebells in front of him, the sun between the dappled leaves and a stream babbling in the background. She tells him if the visualisation doesn't work, to take himself to another place where he feels comfortable, safe.

Her fingers are very tentative, she's scared to put too much pressure on his skin. She's gently massaging his shoulders, easing her fingers into the blades, releasing tension and smoothing his neck in upward strokes. She is rubbing in circular motions between shoulder and neck and squeezes the skin between her fingers, stretching it and letting it go. Ella goes over his head with her fingers circling, loosening his scalp, making sure each area is stimulated, rubbing round his ear lobes, massaging the outlines of his face. She can tell by his breath and tiny little quirky movements reflected in his mouth that he's enjoying the experience. His eyes remain closed.

Ella has gone over his aura. She follows the contours of his body with her hands, a foot or so away from his body; if her fingers vibrate in a certain spot she leaves them until they're still. The whole process is intuitive. She holds her hands over his feet grounding him, as she gets a sense that he's not earthed. At the end of the session she sweeps any negativity away, grounds herself too by putting her palms towards the earth and taking a few deep breaths. She puts her hands back on his shoulders.

If nothing else, Patrick rarely sits still for any time apart from going outside for a ciggie so this is giving him time out, where he is still and focused.

'Now gradually and slowly come back to me. There is no rush, come back from wherever you chose to go, when you are ready and not before. There's no hurry, take your time. Slowly let your eyes open get accustomed to the light and rub the palms of your hands together.'

Patrick stays still for a couple of minutes and then gradually comes back. He confesses, 'The visualisation didn't really work.'

'Thanks for being honest.'

'How did you feel?'

'I realise you allowed me time for myself, for me. My thoughts are all over the place and you allowed me to try and settle the dizziness in my head.'

'That's good.'

'Would you like to try another session next week? Mondays are a good day for me.'

So, this is how the months of healing sessions started.

She begins each session with a massage of his shoulders neck and head. Was she trying gently and surely to get into his psyche, or was this just her natural tactile self? If she was being truthful it was probably a bit of both.

Early Monday morning glows sepia from the street lamps and lights the dark November blanket skies.

Ella's neighbour comments, 'You're up early.'

'Going to see a special friend.'

'Very special friend?'

'Hopefully.'

Ella closes her front gate and walks. Occasionally she rests at a bus stop bench, but keeping her limbs moving is good. She has promised Helen who will soon be leaving the café bar that she will always look after Patrick.

Helen had said, 'Give Patrick a hug and make sure it lasts thirty seconds so the oxytocin is released.' Ella knows promises are something you always keep if at all possible. She has learned that from very early childhood. She cared for Tony until she could do no more; she stretched herself into incapacity.

She passes the familiar landmarks: a school, a Chinese take away, a park and now the café is only five minutes away. On this chill day, the sky lightens to grey; one by one the sepia glows extinguish, as she reaches her destination.

Ella enjoys massaging Patrick's neck, shoulders and face. Now the visualisation she offers him is of golden sands. He's lying there outstretched, his body caressed by the warmth of the sun, sand, or maybe he chooses to dip into the refreshing ocean. This visualisation works better and reminds him of Bali, the beach. Later on, when she massages him fully, he would compare it to the massages he enjoyed whilst on holiday.

'I like the pressure, it's less tentative than when you first started.'

'More searching.'

'Delving even.'

She thought she would love to stop his drinking, which was sometimes excessive. But she just said, 'I enjoy it.'

'Thank you for giving me your time.'

She longed for a hug and had been practising by talking to her pillow, asking him for a hug. She knows he hugs friends and Helen, who was helping him in the café, always hugs him. She promised Helen, she'd look after him. She feels brave.

'Can I have a hug please?'

'Of course.' He hugs her.

Ella feels safe and secure.

He gently lets go.

'I thought you might refuse. I was scared,' she confesses

They look at each other and laugh.

When she goes home she writes a poem.

What Is It?

Holding contoured

shapes in place

resonates self-worth

being cherished

an echo of a childhood

cuddle.

Protected secure

accepted

wrapped in a warm

blanket

surrounded by a

safety net.

Cocooned in a bubble

of happiness

which bursts

when arms, hands

release yet the glow

leaves an imprint

on the brain

reassured accepted

included

treasured

hugged

by friend, lover, family.

Ella continues her Monday morning healing for several months until he sends her a text: 'Sorry, wife come for coffee and chat. To save embarrassment, I'll text u when she's gone.'

Ella goes to the park and sits down. She watches the ducks, and geese honking. It's like a warning grawl. Like the sound of her phone, when his text came through. People stroll round the pond. She buttons up her coat. It is a grey, damp December day. She sits and scribbles in her notebook. She hears her phone: 'She's gone. See u soon.'

They meet. He embraces her and she feels his tremors. He's shaking, but she holds him until the tremors stop. She doesn't know it then, but she's given him his last healing session.

****

To make the clay bowl water-proof she dips it into well-whisked up transparent glaze, ensuring an even surface. The burnished sections will still be highlighted. She likens those parts to her hands that recognise the massage strokes Patrick enjoys. Those shimmering patinas will survive, mirroring how Patrick makes Ella feel safe, makes her glow from inside. The connection is embedded deep within her.

She remembers the feel of his skin beneath her fingers. Totally different but a strange similarity with the joy she found holding her babies. The delight she felt cuddling their toasty, milky, flesh. The joy she experienced touching their bodies, feeling them squirm under the pressure of her fingers. Stroking their skin.

****

Chapter Twelve

Ella recalls offering to clean his café bar floor and Patrick remarking, 'That equates to you washing my underpants.'

Ella likes the analogy. She has never washed his clothes. Not even when he lived with her. She didn't really cook for him either. But she remembers cleaning the paint, the paint that he'd spilled at the bottom of the stairs of the café bar. Ella can remember the conversation completely. It is printed, no, imprinted, into her mind.

'Why don't you just rest, talk to me, just sit and chat.'

But the paint at the bottom of stairs has been annoying her for a long time. Why is she refusing to chat with him? Isn't that what she wants most of all? Yet she doesn't want those eyes to swallow her. She wants to touch him, hug him, but she knows he has other things to do. Her grandmother, who had countless affairs, cleaned the grate when frustrated and felt better being active. She wonders whether some of her granny's genes were pulsating in her now, but quickly put the thought on hold.

'You could do your tax receipts. You remember you told me you should be doing them?'

He compares his tax receipts to photo editing. 'The piles get sorted and they get smaller and smaller as you try and figure out what the photographer really wanted. Why did he go outside and then go inside? You try and follow the thread.'

'Is it difficult to choose?'

'It's a matter of elimination so the piles become smaller and smaller until you can show the artist the one you think captures the moment.'

She notices his eyes are gleaming; they have a different quality than when he's looking at her. He's really alive. She'd been fiddling with the tables in the café bar, making sure there are enough knives, forks, spoons and serviettes.

'Do they often agree with you?'

'Most of the time they do, but not necessarily. They may suggest another picture.' He begins to frown and she turns to him. He comes over to her, squats down beside her. 'Look I don't want to hurt you. There's a definite connection between us. It goes deeper than you think. You know I'm not free.'

'I realise.'

'Believe me. I really love having you around.'

'I would just like some time with you alone, not in this fish bowl but in my place.'

'You know she's the love of my life.'

'I realise thirty years is a long time. I don't want to be another spinning plate.'

'I enjoy your company. I really appreciate you being around, constantly promoting the business. All the things you do for me don't go unnoticed. Please believe me.'

'Getting people to come and visit the place.'

'Enticing people.'

'You're good at being a host. You make delicious food.'

'I'm more than happy to support whatever you do in this venue, whatever the outcome.'

'I'll make sure it's a success.'

'I know you'll do your best.'

'Have you got a wire brush and chisel?'

'What the hell do you want them for?'

'To clean off that paint that got spilled at the bottom of the stairs.'

'For Christ's sake! Just sit down and talk to me.'

'It's a challenge, like blackheads, pressing the skin. They plop out.'

'A perverse pleasure.'

'It's like your brain. It's a total mess.'

'For goodness sake rest! You don't have to do it. I haven't asked you to do it. I was going to do it sometime.'

'It's been annoying me for ages. You can get on with whatever you need to do.'

'It's only been there a few days. I was waiting for the paint to dry and then it would be easier to get off.'

'Bloody hell, it would make me feel better.'

'Well if it's going to make you feel better, how can I refuse?'

'Not as much as fucking you, but that's not allowed.'

'Mind your language.'

'Sorry it just slipped out.'

'That might be difficult… I have problems in that area.'

'Because of drink?'

'Probably. You wanted a chisel and wire wool.'

'Thanks.'

Her body feels energised with the physical work. Patrick goes upstairs to his room which doubles as an office, hopefully to do some administration. She has at least given him the opportunity to catch up with things. Ella thinks of the time when she was going through her divorce with Robert. She was digging a friend's garden and, seeing the ground gradually clear, she felt a sense of progress, even if she couldn't alter the turmoil in her own life. The freshly turned over patch of soil became larger, ready for planting.

Ella scrubs; a lot of the paint comes off, but there are stubborn bits that cling onto the floor. Her arms are aching and hands sore. She wants it totally clean. A pure piece of floor to clarify her feelings: she doesn't want to overstep the mark between friendship and sexuality, nor to give double entendres; she wants to keep the letters compartmentalised, geometric, the way he likes them. Yet she knows, she can just spill words out and feel safe. Ella perseveres, like she will with her novella. She perseveres until the floor is spotless. Patrick comes down.

'What an amazing job.'

'All apart from that bit on the carpet.'

'I'll deal with that.'

The last fragment of memory sparks into her mind when she redoes his room above the café bar. It's full of detritus, even rotting vegetables that he hasn't used for chutneys, or whatever he's planned to make with them. She comes in early one morning, carrying a large carrier bag. It is just before Helen goes travelling. Helen's happy to take charge of the café. Patrick and Ella go upstairs.

'No wonder your brain is mucked up. Look at the mess you are living in. Please get us some black bags, then we can sort out what's rubbish and what you need to keep.' He comes in with a roll of them.

'Let's start with the clothes. The dirty ones in a black bag, please.'

Ella has emptied a plastic container. 'Pass me the clean ones.'

He sniffs each item and hands her the clean ones, which she folds neatly, puts into the container. 'Put the dirty ones in the bathroom for washing.'

The receipts are in plastic trays, which she puts together.

'Now please take the cutlery and china out, put it on the ledge between the kitchen and your room.'

His bedroom side-table, (is that the right word?) is made up of two 'do-it-yourself' boxes on top of each other, full of tools. Ella places a stone with a heart on it. She has painted the words 'You are Special' on it. She gives him an anti-war graphic novel and her mother's black lacquered cigarette box, which is decorated in bright colours. Together they manage to remove the detritus that covers the carpet, next to his narrow single bed.

So he's not looking at mounds of stuff in the eaves, she takes her pieces of Indian material and hangs them up. So, he has a picture of a Buddha, a silky brown and gold piece of material, a brighter piece in reds and yellows at the end; it's a bit of a mismatch but at least provides a temporary barrier to the debris.

The rotting vegetables are binned. The computer table and printer on the makeshift desk are wiped, empty glasses and dirty crockery removed. The jar quarter-filled with coins is dusted.

Patrick comments, 'A pathetic collection of two pounds coins towards a possible holiday.' His shoes are tidied under the bookshelf and the bookcase, put into some kind of order

'Look I found your electric toothbrush.' It was shoved in the bookcase hidden by papers.

'I wondered where it got to,' he retorts. She puts it in the bathroom.

Patrick gets out the Hoover. The carpet becomes more visible and less grim. She climbs on the bed, hangs up his coats hat and scarves. She puts a bedspread over the bed. Moth-eaten clothes are chucked.

'I really liked that jumper.' It was pinkish red and very soft. 'But never mind it can go out with the rubbish.'

He's been compliant and when Helen comes upstairs she is amazed at the transformation. God knows how long he's lived in this mess, probably since his temporary separation from his wife.

'I need to get on with preparing the food now. Thank you so much for your help.'

'I'll be checking it stays relatively tidy. Have a good day.'

'You too, Ella.'

That evening Patrick texts her: 'Hi Ella I'm slumped in bed listening to Eckhart Tolle on audio book. Now that's a change for me! I'm also thinking I need to keep the room tidy – also a change for me. I have you to thank for that. I hope your day was happy. You move in many ways... I'll see u tomorrow and wish you a peaceful sleep. I'll sleep in my suddenly comfortable and strangely spiritual and warm cocoon. Goodnight Ella x.'

The Community Centre, like Patrick, had made her feel comfortable, wanted. She had moved back to an area where she'd started a playgroup when her children were small. The old Community Centre was now a building site. She'd volunteered for a decade in the replacement Centre but now she was dealing with its undecided future. She knows that indecision, not knowing, causes her stress. Not knowing what Tony might or might not do, his continuous vacillations, his unwillingness to put down roots, invest in a house that was theirs, his mood swings from elation to gloom. She knows she needs control.

Ella has made Patrick part of her life. He's given her something precious. He's touched her, held her words, her mind, and at times her body. She likens it to the people she's come across in the Centre, who feel able to express themselves in this space which embraces them, makes them part of the community. The idea and the reality make her feel happy. Her drop-in writing group allows others to discover writing as therapy, a diversion. It's a source of their and her healing.

She knows the group can continue and meet elsewhere if necessary. But it will be different. Ella is being positive, connecting with different people whose voices are often unheard and listening to their stories. Stories give expression to hidden thoughts just as she foretells in her story about Aurora and Zelis.

Ella believes friendships are a form of loving. She is trying to separate friendship from her physical desire. She is learning to be compassionate and trying to practice non-attachment. Not always successfully.

Ella will always be grateful to Patrick for germinating that seed that sprouts on clean paper sheets, unleashes stifled emotions, is contained by duty and care. Now she deserves to be loved by another who loves her equally, hugs her words and cherishes her strength, her vulnerability, her wellbeing. She wants someone who wants to dance in the brushstrokes that tenderly outline her flesh, hold her as a precious pen stroking the page, making beautiful shapes.

Yet she has been tempted by the deliciousness of desire, sometimes so overpowering, cloying, clawing, invasive; and intoxicating like the sweet succulence of lilies whose stamens imprint their perfumed pheromones leaving an indelible stain and recalling a basic physical and natural need. He's pierced through her more than he'll ever know, but he's also let her float new-born.

Meanwhile she gives out her kindness to others, and some to herself. Is it self-indulgent writing this novella? Maybe self-knowledge is empowering? It gives her pleasure, focuses her.

She feels upset that her work is coming to an end. She wants something other than her words to grow, so she reverts to her natural space. Ella's natural space is her garden. She goes to the greenhouse. The wind whirls, the rain pelts bitter cold. She removes the dead debris from the passion plant that's burgeoning over one side of the greenhouse. She shakes the foliage letting the caught, shrivelled, dead leaves fall from their stranglehold of living growth and she tidies as best she can. She opens the clear seed-packets of sweet peas – then plants and waters them in pots in the greenhouse.

She's neglected the greenhouse for a fortnight. It is around Easter now, which seems particularly apt. This is a time for transformation. She feels compelled to plant hope into the earth. She accepts her relationship with Patrick has altered. He only ever wanted friendship from her. Ella wants to make sure the friendship is nurtured. The seeds are unseen, hidden and buried beneath in dank earth. Ella opens other seeds and places them in the borders of the garden; even if a few of these miniscule seeds survive they will give added colour.

This reminds Ella of re-arranging Patrick's room at hers back into a spare room, one where her grandchildren can stay. She changes the sheets, puts the soft toys back at the end of the bed. Story books are neatly placed on the wooden box, which became littered with bits of paper, tobacco, banana-skins, lists, when Patrick stayed with her. He would always be untidy. She smiles.

Ella takes her older grandchild to London soon after she's cleared Patrick's room. They go on the train. Luckily her granddaughter meets school friends on the journey up to town. When they reach the Southbank, they see a free show walk, along the Thames and have something to eat. The highlight is an animated film of *Revolting Rhymes* by Roald Dahl, accompanied by a symphony orchestra who demonstrate how different instruments alter the mood of the animation; an oboe brings pathos, a flute, jollity.

That night, when Ella and her granddaughter come back from London, she tells her bedtime stories and sings her to sleep, a routine she's used for years although her grandchild has reached double figures. She's used the normal ritual, as she was missing her mum. The familiar soothes her granddaughter, just like Ella has got used to being cuddled. After a while her granddaughter's hand that gripped Ella's tightly releases her hold, her breathing eases and the pillow enfolds her sleeping head. Ella is able to creep out, leaving the door ajar.

Ella gets a text from a friend who's not well and feeling vulnerable. She would like to stay with her. Her daughter lives nearby so this way she can see her daughter during the day, but come and rest whenever she needs. How can Ella refuse? The room is empty. It's just for a week and otherwise her friend would have to sleep on her daughter's settee, wouldn't have any privacy.

Ella smiles to herself. Patrick started on the settee at her place as that way he could use the shower room downstairs and the loo during the night, not disturb her, be further away from her bedroom, be separate. Ella had a bathroom en-suite.

She recalls that after the first few days she moved Patrick to her spare room which would be more comfortable for him. He'd said, 'Are you really sure, do I deserve to sleep upstairs?'

She laughs, 'Of course. It's more sensible, as long as you don't mind going downstairs to the loo.' She knows he goes to the loo frequently during the night hours.

She gave Patrick a room when he needed a place and is now going to ask for her key back. Yet she finds herself questioning this. Does she really want to take the key away from him? She knows he'll never use the key without permission. Does she want him to feel rejected or that she is rejecting him? They would never be lovers apart from a passionate flirtation in her head. Ella decides she will let Patrick have the key, as a keepsake. He had unlocked her heart, hadn't he?

It made her reminisce, to when Robert, her first husband, had taken his mistress away and Ella looked out of the window. He'd come back at the end of the weekend with presents for them all. She remembers being given a sage green, glazed, handmade bowl, which she'd wanted to smash in her outrage. She didn't, but she put the bowl at the back of the cupboard, out of sight. Ironically, it proved very useful over the years.

The past was the past and she doesn't want to look back. She likes being focused in the now. Today Ella changes her bedding, puts on a new fitted sheet, reversible duvet cover and pillow cases. She treated herself to these at her weekly supermarket shop. They are an aquamarine and a subtle beigey brown: water and earth mixture – making mud. Mud is where the lotus flower blooms. She looks forward to sliding between the crisp covers later that evening.

Patrick has allowed her to bloom, not staked her; protected her desire, not undermined her; sometimes criticised but he's made her feel beautiful. She still feels beautiful and that shines in the play she wrote as a fragmented story before her novella. Ella was trying to fill the interstices.

The play ends:

The connection remains.

We're still friends

mirrored in the flickering flames

written in this fragmented story –

metamorphosed into broken pieces –

held in a mosaic I can see

of two fish swimming in the same pool

passing in different directions,

glinting from my kitchen window.

They are two fish swimming in opposite directions, both seeking happiness. Ella has not abandoned him, nor rescued him. She's swept him up in a tide of words and let the words reveal her true self, who normally hides between the covers.

This is just for you

my true friend

the one who I can be intimate with

share my innermost thoughts.

Although we will never share the same bed

you penetrate my head

my very being

your root intertwined with mine.

You allow me to shed those layers

stuck fast to me for more years than

I care to remember –

I am as naked in your presence.

I am as comfortable with you

as a second skin.

You pull words from my solar plexus,

your knife guts,

dismembers the pain,

disgust, shame

I was made to feel, felt

about my sexuality –

those thoughts now trashed, binned.

You hold my hand looking

directly at me, sweep that detritus

out of my system

you thank me for saving your life

yet you have touched me,

allowed me to reciprocate

so my skin tingles, is revived.

You make me glad to be alive,

accept my need to be held, cherished.

Please don't worry,

I am strong enough

will be able to cope

when you are gone.

I'll remember your arms around me

and will take each day as it unfolds

write words upon the page

swirl colours on paper

breathe and breathe again.

Like you unfurled the true me

you looked, saw, were seen,

both of us knew self-discipline –

we will follow your advice, keep things simple

not make them complicated

won't fuck things up.

Those precious minutes I lay in your lap

on the edge of sleep

held safe by you

are more than enough

to give me a sense of peace.

Tears are flowing as I type this

tears of joy and gratitude,

it's all I ever wanted from you

and you gave it without thinking,

thank you, Patrick the Piscean.

Ella knows her heart will mend. Her tears will staunch in time, like a tourniquet, a blue plaster; and her fixed outward grin will hide any temporary seepage. Ella realises she must, how would Patrick put it... *hang in there*!

Today Ella's off to storytelling group. Her story is about the plight of refugees, inspired by a production called *Gone*. She remembers the refrain from the performance: 'Everything will be alright.' Her breaths have a hint of laughter, thinking of one of Patrick's texts: 'I promise you everything will work out for the best.'

Ella knows there is just one thing she must do. Yes, he has opened her heart to the possibility of a relationship, but she must protect it. She should ask for her key back. She is responsible for her own heart. He has empowered her and she will always be fond and grateful to him. As her grandmother asked, 'If I planted a tiny seed of love in your heart would you water it and let it grow?'

The answer was, 'Yes, Patrick, you have prepared the ground, allowed me to acknowledge how I do sometimes feel lonely. Now, I'm ready for a relationship.' She thinks of her garden where something unexpected will always take root and surprise her. Mourning tears, like rain, will turn to a sunny, upturned smile.

The day she asks for her key back, he is busy getting things together, doesn't really want to be disturbed, but nonetheless invites her in. She sits quietly as he completes his email and then asks, 'Please may I have my key back?'

'I thought I'd given it you back.'

She smiles, 'No.'

He takes his keys out of his pocket, 'Is this the one?'

She nods. He slips it off the key ring and places it in her hand.

'I'm not rejecting you in any way. I just need it back to move on, protect myself.'

'It's fine. It gave me a feeling of warmth having it.'

'It was really difficult for me to ask you, but I knew it was something I should do, for me.'

'Please don't worry.'

'Can I have a hug please, and then I'll go. I appreciate you're busy.'

Patrick hugs her gently. They kiss each other's cheeks, with the softest of embraces. She goes to the door and he reiterates, 'I'm not kicking you out. It's only I have loads of stuff I've got to get on with.'

Ella smiles, 'I know. I'll be in tomorrow as normal.'

She walks down the street and pops the silver key safely into her bag; zips it up. Her hand touches her mouth, remembers his kisses, his arms enfolding her, wrapping her carefully, sandwiching her in parchment, no – greaseproof paper would be more apt, a take-away. She's taking back her freedom.

Her phone pings, a text: 'The Centre will stay open for another six months and probably after that too.'

The sun shines, her steps are briskly tapping the paving stones.

****

Ella's fingers caress the keyboard, wanting to linger, feel the texture of the words, hoping they'll penetrate, no rather – reverberate like the swooshing of waves on the shore in that momentary pause before they touch the beach, a lull before pulling away or sweeping in. They may choose to caress or crash on Ella's foothold. It faltered but she has kept her balance. She's opened herself to the tide, letting her words spread onto the page.

She has planted seeds in her garden, wanting their coloured threads to sprout hope and happiness.

The bowl is re-fired at a higher temperature so the glaze melts. Patrick has cupped Ella in his hands. She has uncovered her structure, learned her weaknesses and knows that her innate ability to give will never alter. She will endeavour to mediate emotion with reason. Now the burnished bowl is smooth to the touch, has become stronger, protected with a waterproof sheen. Her dormant seed will bloom.

****

Acknowledgements

Ella's pen naturally scribbles a stream of consciousness. She's previously written and performed a play about this friendship. Steve, who works in the theatre, saw the play and wanted to know more about the connection between the characters. This first seeded the idea of writing a novella. Friends Michelle, Lizzie, Vanessa and Charlie have all read 'Between the Covers' in various stages of gestation. She's mulled over their valuable feedback and appreciated their support. She acknowledges her gratitude to all the other people who have inspired her to persevere with her creation.

Dawn Austin Locke, her editor, gave her extensive notes on the first rough outline, asking her to show more feelings and develop the plot, but found enough gold dust to encourage the author to search out the nuggets of truth which would enable the story threads to be spun. Ella was guided by Dawn, an understanding critic, and her inspirational expertise. The writer still maintains her belief in developing her art organically and goes with her gut feelings.

She finds life writing nourishes her like well-rotted compost does the earth. The soil succours those threads hidden underground, fantasies that transform the tap-root to rebirth the shoot and produce a hybrid flower that has been seeded in truth and grown in the imagination.

This special, deep connection allows Ella to slough off her outer skin. The writer releases hidden hurt, desire, humour, philosophy and, in the process, uncovers her reality. Now she must let the worked words go. Let the baby be born. Cut the umbilical cord.

The author will give all the money from her book sales to Cascade Recovery Café, 24 Baker Street Brighton, BN1 4JN, which helps people to reclaim their lives. She recognises that writing 'Between the Covers' has enabled her to find healing too.